Credit

Repair

How to Repair Credit and Remove All Negative Items

(The Ultimate Guide to Improve Your Credit Report & Achieve Credit Repair Quickly)

Larry Heard

Published By **Bengion Cosalas**

Larry Heard

Credit Repair: How to Repair Credit and Remove All Negative Items (The Ultimate Guide to Improve Your Credit Report & Achieve Credit Repair Quickly)

ISBN 978-1-7772550-7-7

No part of this guidebook shall be reproduced in any form without permission in writing from the publisher except in the case of brief quotations embodied in critical articles or reviews.

Legal & Disclaimer

The information contained in this book is not designed to replace or take the place of any form of medicine or professional medical advice. The information in this book has been provided for educational & entertainment purposes only.

The information contained in this book has been compiled from sources deemed reliable, and it is accurate to the best of the Author's knowledge; however, the Author cannot guarantee its accuracy and validity and cannot be held liable for any errors or omissions. Changes are periodically made to this book. You must consult your doctor or get professional medical advice before using any of the suggested remedies, techniques, or information in this book.

Table Of Contents

Chapter 1: Who Keeps Credit Scores?

Even if you are scrolling through Instagram or TikTok, numbers decide whether or not or no longer or not you need a video or not. And I don't suggest the set of rules; as a substitute, it's our choice-making. The reality is, you are more likely to have interaction with a video or follow an influencer based totally on the range of likes, views, or lovers they have got. It's like we stay in a weird episode of Black Mirror. However, those aren't the numbers that without delay have an impact on the lives of masses of lots of Americans. There is a 3-digit quantity that has the electricity to trade your existence for higher or for worse: your credit score score rating rating. But what's a credit score rating? It is a example of the quantity of chance you pose as a ability borrower. In much less complicated words, it tells lenders whether or no longer or now not or not you're a trustworthy payer.

You can be thinking what the difference among a credit rating document and a credit score rating rating rating is. Credit reviews are the records upon which credit score rankings are calculated. Lenders rely upon your credit score score score to make informed selections without entering into-depth into every consumer's credit score file. Think of it this way: You need to recognize and paintings in your credit score document to enhance your credit rating rating. Credit bureaus collect your credit score information to populate their critiques. In the same way, the Fair Isaac Corporation (FICO) collects those opinions to investigate them to calculate your credit score score score.

Now that you realize the difference amongst a credit score document and a credit score rating score, the following query is: What is a FICO Score? I will give you a brief records to make the entirety smooth. FICO created FICO Scores in 1989 to standardize the standards creditors used to decide whether or not or no longer or not or now not to approve feasible borrowers. They came up with a mystery set of policies based totally mostly on 5 metrics.

You can don't forget it like their non-public specific recipe, like Kentucky Fried Chicken. There are one-of-a-type scores available, however none of them have the name of the game formulation. Before FICO Scores had been popularized, creditors did now not have a honest approach to understanding if an applicant have become sincere. The rankings that existed earlier than all used unique metrics. Some of them used obsolete and beside the issue parameters alongside side gender or political association.

How Does FICO Calculate Scores?

Equifax, TransUnion, and Experian give up raw statistics gathered for their credit score reports to FICO, wherein it's analyzed. That information is then represented as credit score rankings. FICO rankings rely on 5 metrics to calculate the rankings: price statistics, the quantity owed, credit rating duration, credit rating combo, and new credit. Each metric is essential for specific reasons and measures fine and terrible statistics contained in your credit score rating record. Because every elegance's significance modifications from individual to character, you may reflect onconsideration on credit score rating rankings like credit rating score fingerprints. Each score is particular to the individual it belongs to. For example, scores for customers which have a quick credit rating statistics aren't calculated the identical way as scores for customers with longer histories. The facts interior your credit score rating document and credit score rating score rankings changes continuously. Fortunately, so do the techniques and the parameters for calculating your score. Due to the regular evolution of these metrics, it isn't possible to anticipate the impact of 1 parameter on your credit score score file. Thus, enhancing your credit score rating rating is truely hard. However, records each of the five necessities is in particular vital whilst you propose to restore your credit score score.

The first of the categories is price records, encompassing 35% of the rating price. They take a look at the variety of past due or omitted payments and the frequency with that you did or did not pay. They take a look at your report for public information which include lawsuits or whether or not or not you filed for economic catastrophe. This section offers notion into your dispositions for making payments on time. They want a complete photo of your commitment, or lack of it, to repaying your debts. The essential reason why charge history is the heaviest of the 5 elements is that it indicates the danger of you paying all over again the whole thing you borrowed. The varieties of payments which may be usually taken into consideration as statistics on your credit score information are credit score rating playing gambling cards, installment loans, finance bills, mortgages, or maybe retail debts.

Second, 30% is primarily based on the quantity of debt you have got were given. Having exceptional balances will boom the hassle of creating different bills on time. Nevertheless, the simply critical detail isn't always the whole stability of your debt, however the credit rating utilization ratio. For example, if a person has not paid off any of their loans and credits them, it method that they may in all likelihood no longer make bills on time, or they may bypass over them altogether. On the opportunity hand, if you owe a large amount of money to a unmarried creditor however are making payments on time for the whole thing else, in all likelihood it acquired't have an effect in your credit score score score score as a whole lot.

The 1/three category is the length of your credit score score records. Usually, the longer your credit score rating records is, the better your rating may be. This metric makes up 15% of your score. This class is reasonably intuitive; the longer you have got got had your money owed open, the higher the impact it's going to have to your credit score rating. These are the primary topics to think about at the identical time as looking into credit score length: age of your oldest account open, the date that you opened your most modern account, the not unusual life of all of your debts, the age of particular credit score payments, and what sort of time has surpassed due to the fact you ultimate used every account.

Fourth, the credit score rating rating combo is calculated thru looking on the styles of credit score score lines you have got got and if you can efficiently deal with them. Credit mix money owed for 10% of your score. You can consist of a aggregate of different sorts of credit score like credit rating score playing cards, retail bills, mortgages, installment loans, and so forth. The cause of this metric is to see how properly you preserve your floor at the same time as dealing with severa types of credit score and the manner correctly you have got were given met your obligations to every of them.

Finally, the 5th metric is new credit rating score. Having a exquisite blend of credit rating is essential, and every now and then we get carried away and observe for specific credit score score . Although this could seem like a outstanding idea, it may portray you as a higher-threat borrower, specially at the equal time as your credit score rating score records isn't prolonged.

FICO Credit Score Range

I actually have pointed out your credit score rating score and the three-digit range that suggestions your lifestyles, now it's time to go deep into the quantity itself. You likely already realise what your credit score rating variety is, however if you don't, let me give an purpose for it to you. FICO Scores range from 3 hundred to 850, and we are able to damage them down into 5 exclusive classes. Sound familiar? These lessons are precise from the 5 lessons we in reality went over, in spite of the truth that. These classes are often utilized by creditors to fast determine your credit score rating score repute. According to Forbes, we can smash down the sorts into:

<580 is taken into consideration a horrible credit score score score, and even as a lender

sees this they may routinely anticipate you are a unstable borrower.

580-699 is underneath the national common, however it's miles visible as a truthful credit score reputation. It way you may be familiar with the beneficial aid of a few creditors, but under unfavourable phrases. For example, you could have better hobby charges than a person with a better rating.

670-739 is at or barely above the national common. If you have were given reached this degree, you've got suitable credit rating and are leaning towards greener pastures.

740-799 is properly above the national not unusual, and it manner you are a low-threat borrower and a responsible payer.

800-850 is taken into consideration remarkable credit score rating, and it takes tough paintings, time, and backbone to obtain this degree. That does no longer suggest it is unreachable, but, and its perks are virtually well worth the attempt (Howard, 2022).

If you don't yet understand your FICO Score, proper proper right here are a few recommendations to help you. Credit card issuers frequently offer FICO Scores to their customers with out cost, so without a doubt test your credit score assertion or their website to find out. Also, a number of them offer this provider even to non-cardholders. You can also go to the FICO internet website without delay and purchase one in each in their three credit rating score score offerings.

FICO Score vs. VantageScore

Both rating systems proportion the equal reason: to inform lenders of the extent of risk a ability purchaser poses. However, they each have specific developments that differentiate one from the opportunity, further to a couple of similarities. FICO Scores had been based in 1989, so that they had been the equal antique for the closing 30 years. On the alternative hand, VantageScore became born in 2006, and it's far owned via the big three: TransUnion, Equifax, and Experian. Since FICO has the gain of getting been round for the cause that '90s, they estimate that no tons less than 90% of lending choices are made with the useful resource of the use of consulting FICO scores (Mercator Research, 2018). Both forms of scores have severa 3 hundred-850 elements, and that they every use the identical five standards for scoring. However, as I said earlier than, they each have their private thriller recipe for weighing those standards. The minimal scoring standards for VantageScore is particular than it's far for FICO. In stylish, it's miles less difficult to qualify for a VantageScore. FICO requires customers to have a tradeline that is six months antique or more, further to each one-of-a-kind with motion over the last six months, at the same time as VantageScore handiest asks for a tradeline with out a selected time period. Fannie Mae and Freddie Mac, government-backed creditors, use FICO for locating out to whom they have to supply loans. However, the fact that some lenders opt for FICO does not suggest that they received't have a look at your VantageScore.

Luckily, the stairs to restore your credit score that we are able to assessment in Chapter three will assist you to reinforce every rankings.

Tradelines

Important requirements to recognize are what tradelines are and the way they paintings. When a creditor approves a borrower for a credit score, a tradeline is created. Tradelines file any hobby related to an account. In other phrases, they song all of the moves you're making even as any sort of credit score is granted to you. The facts enclosed in a tradeline normally includes the choice of the creditor, the form of account or credit score rating rating authorised, the facts of the customer who's answerable for repaying, and the payment reputation.

Other excellent statistics that tradelines song encompass relevant sports activities which incorporates the date the account have become opened or the credit score changed into granted, the credit score score score limit, the price facts, the amount of delinquency if the borrower not on time their bills, and the entire amount of debt. It is vital to factor out that a closed credit score rating account will, maximum possibly, live on a tradeline for as an lousy lot as seven years. Every credit score account has its very personal tradeline.

The price reputation is the most noteworthy information from a tradeline because it illustrates whether or not the borrower has or has no longer made bills to their account on time. If they have truly been on time, the fee recognition will display that the bills are being carried regular with the terms of the agreement. On the other hand, past due bills are grouped in some of days consisting of 30, 60, or ninety. If the lender believes it's far not likely that the borrower pays yet again the debt, and after a positive amount of days, their account reputation can alternate into "rate off." This can also additionally imply that the borrower may additionally moreover additionally have long long past bankrupt.

Thus, it's far steady to mention that better credit score ratings are granted to parties with good-looking tradeline reviews.

To recapitulate, we found that:

A credit score rating rating rating is a 3-digit range inside the variety of 3 hundred-850 that represents your trustworthiness or hazard level as a borrower.

There are 5 requirements that FICO and VantageScore use to calculate your credit score, all of that have precise ranges of relevance. They are:

35% price data

30% quantity owed

15% duration of credit rating

10% credit aggregate

10% new credit score rating

By looking at your credit score score amount, lenders classify you in the following techniques:

<580 is negative

580-669 is truthful

670-739 is proper

740-799 is superb

800-850 is awesome

Tradelines song the statistics in credit debts. Each form of credit score rating rating has its personal exchange line.

Payment reputation is the maximum influential issue of a exchange line.

Closed money owed stay on alternate traces for seven years.

Chapter 2: The Big Three Credit Bureaus

Earlier, I stated that credit score bureaus are folks that create credit score rating evaluations. The industry of credit score rating reporting has existed for around a hundred years. Before Experian, TransUnion, and Equifax have emerge as a detail, credit score rating score reporting agencies had been usually community. It wasn't till the 3 essential credit bureaus slowly obtained nearby companies that they grew into trendy foremost organizations. Credit reporting, moreover referred to as big information, is one billion-dollar agency now. You may be thinking how that organization works. Institutions like banks, shops, financial companies, or maybe landlords are referred to as information furnishers. They percentage your credit pastime with the bureaus for free of charge. The bureaus acquire your credit rating report based mostly on their uncooked information and promote them returned to those identical statistics furnishers.

As I knowledgeable you earlier than, credit score rating reporting organizations collect your credit score hobby and tradelines. Then, they assemble your credit score rating rating report and calculate your rating the use of FICO or VantageScore. Since Experian, TransUnion, and Equifax are called the huge three, they manage your credit score rating score facts based completely totally on the equal requirements but with precise strategies. Therefore, every of the credit score rating opinions emitted is top notch and does no longer include the same data. That is why you need to get yourself up to speed with each of the opinions. Sometimes, the facts varies appreciably from record to file because of the truth the bureaus have high-quality strategies and timelines for while to replace their statistics. Also, data reported to at the least one bureau isn't usually stated to the others. For instance, if a person applies for a modern-day credit score score card, the monetary group will attempting to find advice from actually really one in all your credit opinions, but they may have a favored bureau. Let's say they choose to ask for your Experian credit rating record. In that case, the records of that inquiry will only be available to Experian and now not to the alternative bureaus.

Up until now, you can have had the idea that credit score rating bureaus are all-powerful entities that might seize your records and use it to create reviews without your consent. That is not the case, and that is the only reason that the FCRA end up created in 1970. The FCRA addresses the accuracy, equity and privacy of the statistics amassed and traded through credit score reporting agencies. By now, you recognize that considered certainly one of your rights below the FCRA is free each 12 months access to a credit score document from each of the bureaus. Later, I will give an reason for the outstanding manner to acquire the ones reviews.

TransUnion, Equifax and Experian all use FICO Score 8 for measuring preferred trustworthiness. They use particular FICO

Scores for specific forms of lending. For instance, Experian advanced FICO 2, Equifax makes use of FICO 5, and TransUnion has its very own FICO four.

Let me tell you a few more records about the large 3: Equifax has their headquarters in Atlanta, Georgia. According to their net web web page, they carry out in 25 countries and characteristic an entire of 13,000 employees international (Equifax, 2022). They outline themselves as a international statistics, analytics, and era corporation that caters to unique industries starting from monetary services to government groups. They claim to have a completely unique combo of era and facts assessment that gives you with a completely particular and unique credit score score report. TransUnion is a Chicago-based totally definitely definitely enterprise enterprise and employs around 10,000 people globally. They declare that they see every body as an entire and that they faithfully represent each customer. Experian says they have 20,000 employees disbursed in forty four worldwide places around the arena.

It is right that when assessing creditworthiness, most lenders only test one of the 3 reviews. Yet, it is commonplace for loan creditors to appearance up all three critiques and examine them a good way to make their final desire. This is due to the large quantities of cash at stake. They commonly remember the middle score.

Things You Should Keep in Mind

You can anticipate credit rating bureaus to recognise your name, address, social protection variety, and date of begin. Of direction, they'll be moreover aware about your credit score rating data, along facet your debt, price statistics, credit score score software interest, student loans, and housing statistics. You is probably surprised through manner of manner of all of the statistics the massive 3 very own. For instance, concerning scholar loans, Sallie Mae can document you as delinquent to a credit bureau after forty five days of delayed payments. Typically, federal loans are more lenient and do no longer file till after 90 days.

The Internal Revenue System (IRS) does now not document late profits tax facts to the bureaus. However, if a taxpayer does no longer observe repaying their tax debt to the IRS, or the quantity owed is exaggerated, the IRS can document a federal tax lien. A lien is a prison claim in the direction of the assets of the taxpayer. In other phrases, if you do now not pay the IRS what they're owed, they could claim your house as fee, and this statistics turns into public record. Therefore, credit score bureaus can discover this public information from 1/3 events and add it to your file. Thus, the terrific recommendation I can give you in this situation is to follow the Lannister's motto and constantly pay your debts.

Something else that you must hold in mind is that your rating is continuously evolving. Scoring structures try to maintain up with the current global and its changes, which includes new credit rating rating conduct. Context is essential whilst comparing credit rating rating rankings due to the reality trends change and those spend cash in a distinct way all of the time. Thus, it is ordinary that even in case your credit score rating conduct are steady in the course of a long term period, your rankings can exchange in reality due to the reality calculating techniques trade, too.

Do I Need to Check All Three Reports?

The short answer is 'sure' because of the truth, as I preserve announcing, the statistics inside the reviews modifications now and again, and you could no longer have the identical statistics in all of your reviews. Therefore, you need to be in the understand approximately any possible adjustments which can have each truely or negatively affected your credit rating. Also, you need to ensure the whole thing on the opinions is correct and dispute any data that isn't. If you only hold on with revising and strolling on one record, your score might also improve on that one, but it may, and it likely must, be one-of-a-type on the opportunity . It is probably better or worse, but you'll however need to comprehend so you may also want to enhance them.

In this monetary disaster, we discovered that:

Equifax, TransUnion, and Experian are the massive three credit rating bureaus.

All three credit score score bureaus use FICO ratings but furthermore make use of their private versions.

You need to make your self familiar with all 3 of your credit rating critiques.

Your ratings may additionally furthermore variety notably from one agency to the subsequent.

The IRS does not report to credit score bureaus, however within the event that they file a federal tax lien in opposition to you, that

information may be public and can seem to
your credit score file.

Chapter 3: Simple Steps to Start Repairing Your Credit

So, it's time to capture your device-bundle and duct tape and begin repairing your credit score rating. Now which you understand the inner workings of credit score scores and the three credit score score score bureaus, you may take the important steps as a way to cast off your self from a horrific rating, the use of each trick on your benefit.

But, if you want to recuperation your credit score score rating, you need to understand what it's miles. Fortune shines to your choose, for this records is rather clean to go back with the aid of using.

How Do I Gain Access to My Credit Score?

Although the majority of groups and credit score bureaus employ the FICO device, there are precise credit rating scoring fashions. This manner you may have a one-of-a-kind score relying on the shape of credit score score score modeling that your corporation makes use of.

Consider asking your chosen monetary organization, industrial employer agency, or issuer which sort of credit rating rating model they use. The safe solution would possibly normally be FICO, but there may be nothing incorrect with being thorough and finding out extraordinary credit rating rating corporations' fashions, thinking about that plenty of these scoring models generally generally have a tendency to use many of the equal factors at the same time as they are calculating your rating.

How precisely do you search out your credit score rating rating? There are multiple strategies you could use:

You can test at the side of your loan statement organisation, monetary institution, or your credit card organisation corporation. The majority of credit companies, loan organizations, and banks start out by the usage of presenting you along side your credit rating score score. It can be on a assertion, or you can additionally be capable of get right of entry to it online really with the beneficial resource of logging it into your account.

You ought to make a right away purchase of your credit score score rating score via manner of visiting the three critical credit score rating bureaus right now or via manner of traveling carriers which includes FICO. There is not anything preserving you from the direct source, in any case.

You also can make use of a credit score score score provider or possibly a unfastened credit rating scoring internet web page. The wonders of on line services in no manner prevent, however be cautious what records you offer on free websites. You might be realistic to double-check the legitimacy of the net web site. Other clients clearly revert to paying a subscription fee as a way to have their charge variety monitored.

Besides checking your credit rating, it's miles advised that you test out your credit score document so that you can affirm whether or not the facts supplied is accurate and whole.

By law, you're entitled to collect a loose reproduction of your personal credit score record on an annual foundation, each coming from the three nationwide credit score rating rating bureaus. You can in reality go to www.Annualcreditreport.Com.

Analyzing your credit score score critiques and ratings is probably included in Chapter four of this ebook.

How Do I Analyze My Credit Report?

Reading your credit score score report is one trouble, but facts it's miles a completely terrific cup of tea. You want to address a credit score score file evaluation, but what are the stairs to getting started? This phase will provide an explanation for how to begin.

Contents Within a Credit Report

First of all, what does a credit rating file encompass? You will discover popular quantities of information, each one telling you a few aspect approximately your regular monetary statistics:

Public Record

This a part of the document will encompass any statistics you may have of bankruptcies, judgments, tax liens, and severa other notices you will probably have obtained from the government close to your personal statistics of finance. If you, as a borrower, haven't any public monetary data, then you may discover this precise part of the credit score document to be smooth.

Inquiries

These can be the statistics of any requests made through credit score score rating score businesses to have a examine your, the borrower's, present day monetary facts. The inquiries can fall a few of the clean or hard category, and each may have an impact on your rating in fantastic methods:

Hard Inquiries: These are made by using the usage of lenders who often request credit rating statistics from score organizations when you have made an software for credit rating.

Soft Inquiries: This is while you your self have made an inquiry in your non-public credit score score score record, which need to be performed at least as fast as a yr to confirm that the statistics are definitely accurate.

Collections

This segment may need to include records of all the collections that had to be crafted from you, that would embody:

unpaid debts

statistics of enforcement from groups

not on time bills

repossessions

Anything contained in proper right right here might be pretty adverse to at least one's profile. You is probably taken into consideration a excessive-chance consumer if you had a history of defaults and now not on time payments.

What Negatively Affects Your Credit Score?

Credit scores are determined through pretty pretty more than a few of things. Depending on the options you are making (occasionally without many one-of-a-kind options), your score may be headed in a terrible path. Be searching out the crucial issue factors that play a characteristic in figuring out your common credit rating score score:

Payment History

Your price records is one of the maximum critical additives that makes up your credit score score score rating. Lenders honestly select those who are succesful of getting an fantastic manipulate on their debt and credit score score score money owed. The first rate way to determine this may be to test the credit score records. Considering that people have a propensity to copy their conduct, the fee history is, generally, an accurate reflected photograph of techniques they'll be going to make payments inside the destiny, and whether or not they may be dependable or volatile. What factors of your section information receives concerned? That might be:

car loans

scientific bills

home loan

student loans

cell mobile phone payments

financial institution strains of credit score

save credit score payments

Credit Utilization

"The use of credit score rating" and "credit utilization" searching for advice from the quantity of credit score score you have got available and what's presently being used. To deliver an high-quality instance, when you have a $10,000 restriction on your credit score card and you've got got a $4,000 rate, that would suggest you have got were given used round forty% of your credit score. The credit score score will take a look at all your credit playing cards, similarly in your loans, calculating the complete that you owe. They will then make a evaluation in your credit score score limits. That way that when you have a $10,000 credit score score rating price but you've got $one hundred,000 to be had, your credit rating usage price is only 10%. This manner that you may be checked out in a greater effective slight than in case you absolutely had a $four,000 charge, but you simplest had $10,000 to be had.

Credit Age

Your credit score rating age and your credit score score statistics will replicate how an awful lot experience you have had collectively along with your credit score rating. If you're without a doubt beginning out at the facet of your credit score score score, you can glaringly have much less of a credit score records. If you're new as a credit rating rating holder, there can be absolutely now not an awful lot you may do. However, if you are considering ultimate your credit score score account, you can want to assume two instances. Simply preserving it open and paying a month-to-month subscription might be enough to maintain constructing a dependable credit score record (you certainly need to ensure that you are paying enough into that account to cowl the subscription).

Just one overdue fee, notwithstanding the fact that, can allow your credit rating rating rating to go through. Why? Because your credit score card issuers can be notifying your credit score rating-reporting agencies of this take away, which in flip can knock down your rating.

Applying for Credit

Each time you observe for extra credit, a tough credit score score inquiry is made for your account. Even in case you do not get the credit rating conventional, having this inquiry has some impact to your common credit score rating rating.

Credit Card Accounts

Having too many credit rating score playing playing playing cards open at the same time also can show to be very hard, even if you have been to well pay them on a month-to-month basis. This might probably have an impact on one's potential to borrow cash because lenders need to wonder what might take vicinity if you maxed out all of your playing playing cards. So, try sticking to a few to five credit rating score gambling gambling playing cards, and you shouldn't have a problem.

Use of the Wrong Credit Card

Making use of the wrong credit score score score card can cause issues. You may be thinking what this means; it technique that you want to be cautious which card you are using when you need to make massive purchases. For instance, if you had been going to shop for your self a $500 tv on a shop's card whose max modified into $1,000, however you had already used up $500, then you certainly could in all likelihood have "maxed out your card." But, if you decided to apply a credit score card that had a $10,000 restriction and low utilization, then it wouldn't have as a whole lot of an effect to your fashionable score.

Co-Signing

Co-signing on debt for buddies and family is a brief manner to shatter a robust credit score rating score. Co-signing is in no manner advocated because the debt obligation can show to your report, and in case your family or pals miss even one fee, it'll reflect for your credit score. As you can have guessed, if that charge rolls over to collections, your score is going to pay a heavy rate there, as nicely.

Paying Off the Wrong Debts First

Paying the incorrect debts first can also have an effect. What does this advocate? It approach that you want to prioritize paying any money owed a tremendous way to proper now replicate on your credit rating rating. For example, you may need to pay down credit score rating score card money owed earlier than you pay off an car loan on the manner to get a rating improve.

Ignoring Mistakes on Your Credit Report

Not fixing any errors for your credit score rating record can hurt you. When you are taking a take a look at your credit report (as is usually recommended), you need to take the crucial steps to recuperation your file if you occur to spot mistakes.

In this chapter, we positioned out that:

You have the right to request your credit rating rating from the 3 most important bureaus every year freed from price.

Your public file and inquiries into your file are the most negative on your credit score score.

You can harm your credit score rating score through your price records, credit score age, continuous packages for credit rating score, co-signing, and not paying off your money owed strategically.

Now we dive into what you may count on to discover inner a credit score score document. Depending at the bureau you get your record from, the formatting is probably exquisite; but, each record must at the least incorporate the subsequent five pieces of statistics, which I've certain under.

Personal Information

This will consist of your name, your beginning date, and your social protection huge range. Your file will actually have your preceding and current addresses and all types of contact information, along with your e mail cope with and your phone number. You really need to ensure all the facts on this phase is correct due to the truth even a misspelled name can motive your credit file to be burdened with someone else's.

Employer History

Your credit rating report will consist of your previous employers' further for your modern-day employers' information. Although, this might be blanketed inside the personal information section, relying on the formatting of the credit score document.

Credit History

It could no longer be a credit score record without a credit score score records, and this will be the longest phase of your document as it is taken into consideration the maximum critical. The rating you get to your credit history makes up 35% of your FICO score.

So, on the subject of your credit score score records, your credit rating score report need to, in flip, embody a number of the subsequent objects:

All debts, open and closed, that have been energetic within the very last 7-10 years. These can be character bills or joint debts, so the person that is sharing your account wants to be financially reliable. You have to additionally see topics together with resolved credit score score, domestic equity loans, and pupil loans. It all depends on what you've got been as plenty as inside the last decade.

Payment information. Although the document will no longer include each and each transaction logged in, it'll encompass a record of whether or not or no longer your minimal payments had been on time. Any money owed that are within the poor are a reflected picture of payments that have been neglected.

Names of lenders and lenders.

When the payments were opened and closed.

Your account popularity. You can see whether or not or not your money owed are listed as open, paid, closed, transferred, refinanced, or foreclosed.

You really want to take some time looking through all of your account information, specifically the information. This is in which maximum errors are made. Make sure the credit limits and specific mortgage quantities are updated. This is crucial due to the truth if the credit score rating limit is listed as lower than the one you definitely have, it will harm your credit score rating score usage, which, in flip, will damage your credit score score.

Public Records

Other feasible problems need to embody:

closed money owed which are said to be open

open money owed which can be said to be delinquent

late bills which you really paid on time

wrong dates

a single account this is noted more than one instances

Then, you'll have your public records, which can embody all your debt, bankruptcies, repossessions, and foreclosure. This segment can in reality harm your credit score rating

rating, however it does now not consist of topics which consist of divorces, lawsuits, arrests, or infractions with the law like dashing tickets (or whatever else that would no longer be affiliated together together with your credit score rating score).

Public facts can in reality harm your credit score score rating, so be cautious.

Credit Inquiries

It's important to test who has accessed your records. If you notice too many hard inquiries, it is able to honestly be an instance of identification theft, specially if it's far an inquiry you aren't acquainted with. So, take a look at the dates and the times.

If you discover any mistakes, you should dispute them, especially because of the impact they may need to your credit rating score. Later on, you may learn how to dispute the ones credit score score critiques if mistakes need to arise.

But for now, it is time to test the particular myths that come up at the same time as humans are attempting to find to healing their credit score score file.

In this bankruptcy, we observed out:

How to take an in-depth have a have a look at your credit score rating rating rating

That mistakes are without difficulty made, and which you want to double check the whole lot

Chapter 4: Busting The Most Common Credit Repair Myths

The more you examine, the more you earn. – Warren Buffett

These days, myths run rampant, and wrong data can do an entire lot of damage. When it includes subjects of finances, you can come face-to-face with powerful 'facts' which is probably told over and over all over again but, in fact, are myths. Just as you ought to recognize that cracking one's knuckles can't purpose arthritis, proper right here are the pinnacle myths that want to be busted concerning credit score repair:

Paid Accounts Do Not Automatically Disappear From Your Credit Report

Just because of the truth you paid off your debt doesn't propose that it will certainly vanish out of your credit score score score document. You have the right to honest and accurate reporting, due to this that it ought to be eliminated as quickly as you have got were given paid the collection business enterprise.

However, this is not usually the case. This is whilst you could want to step in and dispute an item. There is a brilliant threat that it will likely be eliminated.

Credit Bureaus Do Not Make Mistakes

Every device is administered thru human beings, and a few component run through human beings is going to have flaws. So, however the reality which you might be tempted to in reality leave your credit score opinions in the credit score score bureaus' arms with out going over the data, the hassle is that errors can though be made. If you bear in mind the quantity of credit reports they need to provide, then there are sincerely going to be errors that might slip thru once in a while, and sadly, a mistake can have an intensive impact in your credit rating rating. So, typically take a look at your credit rating rating critiques on an annual basis, and you will be doing your self a global of favors.

This might in all likelihood come off as startling, but alternatively, no gadget is proper. If there has been a one-duration-fits-all gadget, then definitely every body could be the usage of it. But much like some thing else, the credit score rating can not take all your existence conditions into consideration. Many human beings are underneath the have an impact on that a credit score score rating report is generally accurate, however mistakes can appear.

Closing All Your Credit Accounts Will Boost Your Credit Score

This is an automated no. Having too many lines of credit rating can do an entire lot of damage in your credit score score, so when you have them, shouldn't you be very last all of them?

That is probably a no, and a large one! One rule for price range and existence in favored is by no means to go to the extremes. Taking drastic measures will make you appear as an volatile and unreliable borrower, and lenders can also reconsider lending money to you in the occasion that they suppose you'll possibly truely turn spherical and move lower back to your phrase. The older your credit rating debts emerge as, the greater incredible the effect they'll have on your score. So, in case you maintain a credit score rating account open for an prolonged time frame, it might be a demonstration of accurate economic balance. If you close up up an vintage account, it is able to lower the average of your credit score rating score which might turn spherical and slap your credit score rating right back off. Although last down one or of your most modern-day debts may not be a lousy idea, bear in mind that your intention is to accumulate your credit facts. So, try to keep at the least taken into consideration one of your credit rating money owed.

Early Repayments of Loans Will Boost Your Credit Score

Again, this doesn't truly assist your credit score rating. In fact, making pre-bills now not often has any impact to your score in any respect. If you make a decision to pay off your installment in advance than agreed on, it obtained't automatically mend your credit score rating. In reality, specialists propose which you preserve your debt open, and pay it off reliably on a month-to-month foundation till the settlement is whole. Using this tactic, you will construct a organization and sturdy reputation, proving for your capability lenders that you are inside the addiction of reliably paying off your debt with hobby as agreed upon.

Consider it this manner: Creditors are a organization, and that they make the maximum of your interest. If you don't pay in any other case you repay too rapid, then they are those who end up dropping.

All Credit Reports and Scores Are the Same

Although the bulk of financial establishments use FICO, not all credit score rating score opinions and rankings are exactly the equal. There are other credit rating scoring corporations, and they might take different subjects into interest in terms of your credit score. So, it might be smart to make your self familiar with the exceptional credit score score score businesses. This is due to the truth if you become trying to use an business enterprise that uses a credit rating file and score commercial enterprise business enterprise this is special from the standard, you'll want at the manner to adapt and recognize how they run and what they attention on as regards to the score. That way, it could mirror your financial function within the notable possible mild.

Credit Repair Does Not Actually Work

You can also thoroughly be given as authentic with in credit restore, or you is probably analyzing this ebook however not without a doubt provided on the idea that it might absolutely art work. However, humans have tried these strategies time and again, and feature time and time once more discovered themselves getting out of financial problem through the use of the use of specializing in repairing their credit score score. So, do not forget, start off with reviewing and reading your credit score score record, and then turn to repair mode, solving any inaccurate or incomplete facts that might be for your report, please bear in thoughts to have staying energy. Credit restore isn't always a one-day, brief restore state of affairs. It takes a powerful quantity of time.

The decrease your credit score is, the greater time it is going to take. However, when you have a lower rating, you have got were given a higher risk of boosting your score than if you have a better score. In that case, you will have to change the larger behavior that had been bringing your credit score rating down.

You Cannot Repair Your Credit Completely on Your Own

This is honestly a myth, considering that your movements are important to numerous factors of credit score restore. The more attempt you located into making better and wiser economic options, the extra and greater excessive terrific the have an impact on in your credit score may be. So, keep in mind no longer to take out too many loans, continuously make your payments on time, and learn how to get a grip on your spending behavior.

Credit Bureaus Are Federal Agencies

Many humans have come to simply accept as authentic with that credit score bureaus along with Experian, TransUnion, and Equifax are owned by means of way of, controlled, or come what can also beneath the manage of the federal government, and they discover this regarding. This is, in fact, a fable as credit score rating bureaus act as personal, for-earnings organizations. Although they need to comply with diverse pointers and regulations, they are by no means under the manage of the federal government, and so that you must not be worried approximately this.

Bankruptcy is Your Only Choice

You might probably reap a point wherein you located you have not any exceptional desire than to file for monetary break. However, this have to most effective be used as your absolute ultimate motel. Bankruptcy is probably capable of provide you a brief healing after going via a devastating and horrible monetary scenario, and your credit score rating can also take a amazing, long term to really get over this scenario (nearly a decade). However, earlier than you even come close to selecting financial damage, you want to bear in mind your regular economic scenario. You ought to test every single opportunity or even speak alternatives with a knowledgeable credit score counselor who may suggest answers which you didn't even understand about. A credit score rating counselor can usually provide you with accurate path regarding your monetary sports.

You Cannot Dispute Anything That Might Show Up on Your Report

The real horror can also moreover get up while you recognize there can be a mistake for your credit rating record, and some may also even skip so far as to consider that they're not allowed to dispute it. However, as said in advance than, the accuracy of your credit rating document isn't always confident, or maybe the companies who create them understand this. So, in case you discover an mistakes, acquire the crucial proof, and report a dispute. You want your credit score score rating to stay as accurate as viable on your famous advantage. Otherwise, your credit rating score score won't swing in your choose.

Once You Have a Bad Credit Score, It Will Haunt You Forever

Your credit rating score isn't always a ghost, and your financial statistics will not be found out in your document all of the time, mainly in case you are making wonderful adjustments at the way to swing you proper proper into a immoderate great mild. Although it would take time to recover from a lousy credit score, your credit score rating score will not live caught in a horrible mild forever, in particular in case you're intentionally running on making the vital changes. It is all a consider of attitude and staying electricity.

Before you panic over what you've got a take a look at online (specifically on social media), ensure to constantly confirm the information you get keep of. While we have get right of access to to lots facts approximately budget from across the area, that does not imply that all the information supplied is accurate. The superb manner to decide the fact, especially in phrases of your credit score score, is to the touch the economic enterprise commercial enterprise organisation itself or to the touch specialists who can provide recommendation. Double-check the assets of information which you are becoming your facts from, and ensure it is not only a few blogger seeking to stir up panic. Clickbait is a very not unusual phenomenon that has precipitated humans to panic and make assumptions even in advance than analyzing the object in question. More frequently than no longer, the information in articles supplied with clickbait titles tones down versions of the headings they supply.

Now that we've got addressed all the myths, permit us to dive into topics that can simply negatively have an impact for your score. You need to be aware about those data as you continue to repair your credit score rating score.

In this financial disaster, we determined that:

Accounts you have were given paid off will not proper now disappear from your credit score document.

Every credit rating gadget does now not art work in exactly the same way, however credit score repair is a valid way of fixing your monetary events.

You ought to wait until all else fails before the usage of for financial ruin.

Bad credit score score rankings will now not hold close-out you for the rest of your life, no matter the fact that it could make an effort to restore them.

Chapter 5: Things You Do That Negatively

You have to benefit control over your coins or the dearth of it will all the time control you. − Dave Ramsey

The most damaging threats on your credit score score are horrible conduct. Making one or mistakes collectively collectively with your charge range isn't continually the stop of the area, however terrible conduct are the identical errors being made time and again another time. Bad credit scores do no longer usually upward push up inside a day, but over time. The identical can be stated approximately an outstanding credit rating rating. In order to repair a damaged credit score, you could need to turn out to be aware of all your horrible behavior and hobby on converting them into extra immoderate outstanding conduct. This economic catastrophe identifies the ones horrible conduct.

Late Payments

It is easy to overlook all your subscriptions and payments that need to be made. It can feel like cash is being vacuumed from your financial institution account. Not retaining tune of your bills that need to be made is via manner of a long way certainly one of the most essential errors you can make on the subject of your credit rating. Generally, your charge information is the most important criteria with reference to your credit rating rating rating.

Late payments are actually one in all the biggest factors that may drain your credit rating score. The hassle is that late bills can take region so especially with out problems. Depending on in which you're in lifestyles, the kingdom of your financial institution account, and the effectiveness of your charge range, if you emerge as overspending and end up with a past due price, you're doing your self no favors the least bit.

Bankruptcy

This want to surely not be a awful addiction, and economic destroy need to first rate be a closing motel. It is taken into consideration a monetary Armageddon for a motive. The properly statistics is that it doesn't depart a everlasting black stain in your price variety; but, improving from it may take a excellent while longer than looking for specific viable solutions. Bankruptcy is, in essence, a change-off as it wipes away all of your debt or as a minimum reduces what you cannot manage to pay for to pay, however it does declare to the location that you are certainly a big credit rating danger. When monetary disaster suggests up in your credit rating record, it sinks your credit score rating rating dramatically. It will become extra difficult, if no longer impossible, to each borrow and spend for a powerful term. You want to stand immoderate hobby fees, shorter payback instances, and quite some mortgage rejections. Depending on in that you are in existence and what you want financially, this will cripple your commonplace financial scenario and properly-being. So, once more, you need to virtually anticipate two times, or perhaps 4 to five times, in advance than you're making this preference.

Less Diverse Credit Mix

Although having a much less severa credit score rating rating isn't always altogether a assure that you could have a decrease credit score score score, the greater high-quality sorts of credit score score rating you've got, the higher. So, what's a credit score score mixture? This is all your wonderful varieties of credit score money owed that are used to calculate your credit score ratings. This element is often ignored. For example, you will likely have a mortgage, a non-public mortgage, a pupil loan, and a credit score score card, which makes a wonderful credit combination that might deliver human beings a better idea of your personal rate variety and common reliability.

So, when you have a miles much less diverse portfolio, it could no longer motive your scores to move down, but it acquired't usually assist in your repair both. However, a cautious balance is wanted right here. It is good to have a numerous credit score rating score combination, but too many bills also can reflect negatively on you, particularly if a number of your open debts are the same form of account.

Applying for a Lot of Credit in a Short Time Span

Every time which you request a credit score rating score report due to the fact you've applied for a loan, you could have a hard inquiry logged into your credit file. These inquiries can definitely live for your file for over years, and they could cause your score to falter and pass down barely for a fantastic time frame. Lenders pay specific hobby to the difficult inquiries as it is an illustration of ways hundreds new credit score rating score you're figuring out to request. If you request too many internal a brief-time span, it may suggest that you are absolutely suffering financially or that you are being denied new credit score score score from distinct economic establishments. Neither shine very favorably for your score.

Impulse Buying

Impulse shopping for is clearly certainly one of the biggest offenders which could lead you immediately into credit score score debt, the usage of an excessive amount of credit score rating rating usage, and, ultimately, lowering your credit score score score. What is impulse buying, moreover known as impulse spending? It is buying a few detail that you were not planning on shopping for. The company global of advertising and marketing flourishes on this workout. Here are some steps you can take to keep away from impulse spending:

Delay your choice. Whenever you encounter a few detail you would like to shop for, typically put off your choice. You need to postpone with the useful aid of hours or two days; the point is to keep away from making any sort of hasty buy. The more time you supply your self, the more rational you'll be at the same time as you come upon the same services or products another time.

Use purchasing lists. It's a reduction, so I am saving, right? Well, no longer virtually. Oftentimes, I encounter extremely good gives, and I take benefit of them, questioning they're a steal. But the problem is that once I walk out of the shop, I turn out to be having spent extra than in the beginning planned. So, every time you want to hit the shop, make a sturdy purchasing listing. Whenever you stumble upon a few element you would love to shop for, don't forget whether or not or no longer you really need it or in fact need it.

Use cash in place of credit score. Using coins is specifically smart in shops wherein it's miles difficult to workout strength of will in the purchasing for of products. When you've got were given a restrained amount of money, you may want to restriction what you buy.

To sum up, constantly have a price range and a shopping list, and stick with your plan every time you go shopping. However, that is very easily said however no longer so with out hassle performed. But, focusing hard on incorporating those habits (on the identical time as leaving a few room for your rate range for desires) will absolutely be definitely really worth your whilst on the subject of enhancing your credit score score rating.

Service Accounts

Service payments, in conjunction with utilities or cellphone payments, aren't automatically protected in your credit score record. In the beyond, credit rating ratings could satisfactory mirror your utility account if the account had been handed on to a set employer. So, ensure to make your payments on time, and avoid getting the attention of series organizations if the least bit feasible.

However, you should note that this is absolutely changing now as a contemporary product referred to as "Experian Boost" lets in clients to get credit score rating for paying utilities and telecom money owed on time.

So, thru the use of Experian Boost, clients are capable of see their FICO Score increase interior certainly mins of the usage of it. This is the exceptional manner of getting greater credit rating score for your software and telecom payments.

Focus on a Budget

The wonderful way to turn topics round to your credit score rating rating might be to devise. The top notch form of monetary making plans is usually a price variety. If you learn how to make a proper price variety and stay with it, you then are forging a a hit route. In fact, if greater humans centered on right budgeting and avoided overspending and getting trapped in overwhelming quantities of interest and debt, then the world's financial device may additionally already be in a miles higher area.

A price range also can provide a realistic image of the manner a good buy debt you could repay on a month-to-month foundation, as well as how a bargain you need to your desires while now and again slipping in goals if your earnings affords you sufficient leeway to achieve this.

And on the subject of your credit rating score, generally ensure to:

Pay the payments you've got were given were given on time.

Pay down the amount of debt you have got got were given.

Cover your amazing payments.

Dispute any form of defective statistics for your document.

Your credit score score, counting on your conditions, will truly take time to get higher. Or, your credit rating score might not be in this form of terrible scenario, however you need to have it boosted. Either way, you need to make cautious choices. Some factors can not be averted with regards to one's credit score rating ratings, but the majority of them can.

So, relying in your scenario, make the effort to surely think about the money you want to apply and the way exactly you need to apply it, and avoid behavior like overspending. Although it is straightforward to vicinity it into terms, setting this into motion is an entire different tale.

In this financial disaster, we placed out that:

It may be very easy to drag your credit rating down by way of way of creating payments past due or via falling into the trap of impulse spending.

You want to tempo the amount of credit score score you ask for over an extended term.

You should cognizance on putting off lousy monetary conduct.

Chapter 6: Fcra Section 609

Financial freedom begins with properly conduct. —Rebecca & Tiago

The FCRA is some other a part of the credit score score score worldwide that many human beings aren't even aware of, however it has the functionality of being your quality pal in case you understand the manner to wield it nicely. Some topics honestly must be handled as though they have been a war.

What Is the FCRA?

The FCRA stands for the Fair Credit Reporting Act, which have become designed thru way of the federal workplace that regulates each the gathering of people's personal credit rating rating statistics and the get admission to humans should their credit score rating score critiques. It turn out to be handed in 1970 to cope with the want for privacy, accuracy, and fairness inside the collection of people's non-public records. The facts is held in documents in the credit reporting corporations.

How the FCRA Works

So, what does it in reality do? Well, it maintains the peace and makes the arena of rate range honest normal. The federal law has a big say when it comes to topics of the collection and reporting of the credit score score facts that it receives. It additionally determines how prolonged the information can be saved and the way, precisely, the records may be shared with others.

There are policies in region regarding the quantity of statistics that can be acquired, how prolonged the information may be stored, and the manner it is able to be shared. The Federal Trade Commission (FTC) and the Consumer Financial Protection Bureau (CFPB) are the two federal businesses which is probably specially in rate of overseeing in addition to implementing all the provisions within the act. You can locate the act in United States Code Title 15, Section 1681.

Equifax, TransUnion, Experian, and exclusive specialised organizations, all need to abide through the usage of the FCRA when they artwork and promote facts associated with an individual's economic information.

Special Consideration

The FCRA has described in element virtually what form of records the bureaus are allowed to collect. This includes topics which incorporates a person's popular bill charge statistics, the past loans that they have got had, and the present day-day money owed they currently maintain.

They might also gather employment statistics, a person's present and previous addresses, and information approximately whether or not or not or not a person has ever filed for financial disaster, owes little one resource, or has any kind of arrest document.

The FCRA limits folks that are allowed to peer credit score rating evaluations, and similarly they decide underneath what instances a person is permitted to look credit score rating score reviews. The maximum not unusual example can be even as a lender requests to see the report because of the fact someone is utilising for a non-public mortgage, a automobile mortgage, a mortgage, or a few exceptional form of credit score score rating. Insurance groups also are allowed to view a client's credit score record once they exercise for a insurance. Finally, the authorities is permitted to request the data in response to a court docket docket order or if a grand subpoena has been issued. Any character that has furthermore been using for a particular government-issued license also can accumulate a credit report.

And in positive instances, you'll probably provoke a transaction or settlement in writing earlier than the credit rating bureau may launch your record. A splendid example can be if a prospective corporation asks to look your credit score document. They are handiest able to acquire the file in the event that they have the permission of the mission applicant.

Keep in mind that the FCRA states that if someone tries to tug your credit score record, they want to specify the particular motive. The cause could be a mortgage request, severa employment skills, or in truth a landlord seeking to carry out a credit check. If your credit score rating score report is used for impermissible use, then this will be in direct violation of the FCRA.

What Are Your Rights?

Naturally, you've got the right to peer your very own report. It is your personal records, anyhow, and through way of way of regulation, you're entitled to get keep of a free credit rating file yearly from each of the three credit score bureaus referred to proper proper here. You can request the file from AnnualCreditReport.Com or from the credit score bureaus themselves.

According to the FCRA, you also are allowed to (2018):

Verify your document and check the accuracy, specially in phrases of topics of employment.

Receive a specific notification each time your record is getting used whilst you're utilising for credit score rating rating or different forms of transactions. This way, you could additionally grow to be aware of even as your credit score report is getting used for impermissible capabilities.

You are allowed to dispute and ensure that bureaus correct any defective or incomplete records on your credit file. This is specifically accessible whilst you want to restore your credit score score.

You are allowed to have any antique and terrible facts removed after seven years inside the majority of times, or after ten years in the case of filed monetary catastrophe.

But what takes vicinity if the credit bureau fails to comply together with your request in a manner that is super? Well, you could report a grievance with the CFPB.

A Good Example of the FCRA in Action

Imagine you are attempting to rent a brand new rental, however the landlord has decided to disclaim your utility. The purpose why they denied it become stated to be your credit score rating score rating. You suspect this to be a lie, and receive as true with it's miles because of discriminatory motives.

Under the FCRA, you are able to request to appearance your credit rating file and verify whether the owner's claims are valid or within the occasion that they lied (they may not surely have pulled your credit score score rating). If you notice a violation occurring, the owner may also need to stand a nice.

The Requirement for Reporting within the FCRA

The FCRA very especially calls for everybody, whether or not or now not or not it's far an insurer, agency, or any other person who is searching for your credit score score report, to have every a legal and a permissible motive to advantage this. The FCRA moreover explicitly states that any awful credit score rating records older than seven years desires to be removed. Any economic disaster can be eliminated amongst seven and ten years after, relying on the form of economic disaster that has been worried as some are worse than others.

What Happens When Companies or Individuals Do Not Comply With the FCRA?

Each violation that occurs can be followed with a excellent amongst $one hundred and $1,000. This might be mainly relevant if any styles of damage had took place or been imposed, which incorporates legal professional charges.

If any individual knowingly received the data beneath fake pretenses, they will even face crook fees.

FCRA Section 609 Explained

There are a whole lot of conditions at work within the FCRA; but, it's far crucial to carry phase 609 in your interest. What is segment 609? Well, it regards dispute letters.

If you've got were given had a awful credit score rating rating for a while, it is viable which you have already heard approximately section 609. Section 609 is a credit score rating restore letter tactic that requests that credit score bureaus dispose of horrible entries that have lingered for too prolonged on your credit score report. It is particularly named after section 609 of the FCRA. This is under the federal law, and it's far included there to shield people from any shape of unfair credit score score and series practices.

If you take a look at the FCRA Section 609, you'll see that it doesn't make any point out of disputes. However, it gives enough facts to build up all of the data for your credit rating score report as a way to schooling session your credit rating score score your self.

609 Dispute Letter

So, how do the ones letters artwork, precisely? Let's start out with a few smooth steps. Although you wouldn't count on to appearance many errors in your credit report, mistakes do happen on occasion.

The bigger problem is the reality that errors on your credit score score rating file take place more often than you observed, and also you need to take the essential steps to relieve some of the bad scores on your everyday credit score score rating.

Generally, a number of the maximum commonplace mistakes humans stumble upon are statements that an account is open whilst, in reality, it's far closed. Delinquent or fake debts also are said at the same time as in fact, they will be no longer delinquent inside the slightest. Worse but, your credit score score document ought to in all likelihood display lacking credit score rating score card bills at the same time as you apprehend and can show for a reality that the vital payments were in reality made.

These mistakes all upload to the reality of why such quite a few Americans are suffering from low credit score rankings. If they decrease your credit score a piece too much with the resource of mistake, you is probably averted from acquiring a miles-wanted loan or an software for a credit score rating score card. Even in case you are capable of draw close a loan, you can have a excessive interest rate connected to it and lots much less mercy in phrases of repayment intervals. So, taking the essential steps of getting rid of the terrible or perhaps unverified entries contemplated on your document is one of the handiest techniques of credit rating repair that might proper away exchange the direction of your credit score rating score. In this example, there are not any lousy behavior to change and no gadgets to head again; there can be without a doubt an alternate and removal of statistics that have become no longer at the start supposed to be there in the first place.

Credit Bureaus

So, it's far easy that credit score bureaus have incredibly important jobs. It is of their palms to create correct and accountable opinions. They determine a big amount of your monetary life and well-being as a mortgage can sometimes provide a person absolutely sufficient to preserve their commercial enterprise going, get thru a phase of unemployment, or address a medical emergency.

Under the law, they want to reputation on which incorporates established and accurate information for customers almost about their credit rating reviews. But this is not continuously the case, and the majority of people aren't even aware about how with out problem errors can slip via the cracks with horrible outcomes.

Section 609 of the FCRA

Section 609 of the FCRA outlines the rights of a customer with reference to subjects of credit score score reporting. Section 609 of the FCRA offers people get admission to to the belongings of data indoors their credit rating documents, and in addition they have the proper to comprehend who exactly accessed their credit evaluations in the very last years. So, it is constantly a fantastic addiction to check up on folks who are checking you out.

Not nice are you allowed access to facts, however you could moreover take the essential steps to clean your credit score record by means of sending them a 609 letter, setting ahead your criminal proper to alternate your credit score facts if there are inaccuracies or incomplete records.

Dispute Letter

This is the technique utilized by folks who need to eliminate erroneous or defective objects from their credit score score opinions. 609 letters are frequently known as dispute letters, however technically, they do not dispute any information. That facts might be blanketed in sections 611 and 623 of the FCRA.

The whole idea within the once more of a 609 letter is the reality that if credit score bureaus cannot provide you with the data required to confirm a credit score debt in your credit score rating document, then they want to get rid of that information out of your credit score report. So, basically, a 609 letter is the place to begin to offer you with enough evidence to create a have a look at-up letter to dispute any erroneous statistics through sections 611 and 623.

What Can 609 Letters Not Do?

There are amazing subjects that 609 letters are not able to doing. For instance, they will be now not criminal loopholes you may use to put off correct bad statistics from your credit score score file. So, even though you may not similar to the document on the file, and as heaps as any mother and father would really like to wipe it out, 609 does now not offer you the avenue to accomplish that. As prolonged as the credit score bureau can verify your debt, that debt will continue to be to your report till a wonderful amount of time has passed seeing that you've were given paid the debt off; notwithstanding the truth that the debt is proven, you could have vintage debt eliminated from your document.

How to Write a 609 Letter

You do no longer must begin truly from scratch, but it's far critical to focus at the formatting and wording of this jail report earlier than sending it. But, don't fall for the letter template furnished through the usage of some corporations; they usually tend to say that they work higher truly due to how the letter is formatted.

However, this isn't a first-class-company fiction book or a cowl letter for an interview. You need to take these steps cautiously:

Start off with the resource of manner of requesting your loose reproduction of your credit score score score record, and check for any fake or faulty horrific devices. You actually need to move big with this depend.

If you've got were given determined matters for your report which you would love to dispute, format a letter providing the subsequent facts:

your private records

your criminal professional's facts

the account extensive variety that you have with the credit rating rating bureau

the assertion keeping your FCRA rights which is probably held within Section 609

the gadgets you need more statistics about

your most contemporary-day credit document

your evidence of identity

a request for the elimination of specific records, in particular in the occasion that they can't affirm the object (you may request for them to have it eliminated within 30 days) references to enclosures (the files you sent to the credit score bureau which is probably connected with the letter)

Mail or electronic mail your 609 letter, and make sure it is certified mail that has a go back receipt. Make positive you furthermore mght have a reproduction of the letter you're sending, as well as a duplicate of all the files you want to deliver to the credit bureau.

Although you're greater than welcome to draft the letter with the resource of your self, when you have the capacity, are in search of expert advice from a credit counselor or a credit score repair prison expert. This is particularly applicable if you are unusual with the numerous formal correspondence and technical financial jargon that tends to pop up while interacting with credit score rating bureaus.

Next, it's going to probably be the credit score score bureau's duty to reply and evaluation all of the inquiries (specially inquiries that have 609 letters internal of them). You must be notified of the results all indoors 30 to 45 days of sending your letter. That approach that during case you're requesting files, you ought to get maintain of them inner 30 to 45 days (so, mark the date you sent your letter to your calendar).

Do Dispute Letters Really Work?

We have all seen human beings complain over valid elements, but not something changed. That may additionally additionally suggest that you may clearly shrug it off and not fight the errors no matter the harm it may do.

The trouble is that there may be no assure that a 609-dispute letter will absolutely help you get the awful records eliminated. But it will can help you to get the dispute approach started. The bureau might probable put off the devices in your credit score score score document in case you deliver the letter, however this isn't always a guarantee. When you request the information, they need to offer you with the information you are asking for.

If you discover that the credit score bureau does not respond to your 609 letter or the observe-up letters that you supply, then you can document them to the FTC. This is the enterprise that is in rate of ensuring credit score bureaus look at the law. When you document a grievance with the FTC, you area greater pressure on the credit rating rating bureau. You may additionally see a reaction and they may even go up to now as to restore the mistakes on your document.

Sometimes the ones structures and those take probabilities absolutely because of the truth they keep in mind human beings will not perform a little issue. So, regardless of the truth that dispute letters may not be a strong, set-in stone plan, inaction will thru a long way motive greater harm for your credit score rating score than stepping in and doing what you may to enhance your credit score rating rating, while walking on a sincere or maybe playing challenge.

So, to conclude, despite the reality that the 609 letters are diagnosed to not paintings right away, they may be the high-quality way to get commenced with offering you with the statistics for any dispute letters you may want to deliver to the credit score rating bureau in the destiny. When you draft them truely, the bureau could likely step in and take away the gadgets that have been tested to be incorrect.

If they don't respond, bear in mind to maintain copies of all of the requests you ship. These will assist you for your road inside the course of your dispute. But, consider that the 609 letters aren't loopholes so you can cast off all awful credit score score score. They are actually there to accurate errors and inaccuracies. So, while you look at your document, make sure to double-check whether or not or not or not you have got truly noticed a mistake.

Apart from having a awful credit score removed, it's time to awareness on distinct actions you can take that allows you to enhance your credit score rating score, that is what you'll be learning inside the next financial disaster.

In this bankruptcy, you determined that:

The FCRA is the federal place of business that collects the credit score score score information of every man or woman.

You have the proper to request your document on an annual foundation, and you can affirm it for accuracy and mistakes.

You are allowed to request that any antique data or errors be eliminated after seven to ten years.

The FCRA Section 609-dispute letter is in which you could inquire approximately the information for your credit score rating record to affirm the information recorded on it.

Dispute letters cannot cast off facts that can be tested.

Chapter 7: Boosting Your Score

The pace of your fulfillment is restrained only thru your strength of mind and what you are inclined to sacrifice. –Nathan W. Morris

Now which you understand what you need to keep away from, it's time to check the steps you can take to make sure that you could formally decorate your rating. After all, your purpose isn't best to remove horrible economic conduct, but additionally to feature right monetary behavior with a purpose to keep you slowly however absolutely repairing your credit score score.

The Reality of a Low Credit Score

If your rating is an awful lot lower than you would really like, you'll likely virtually be capable of upload one hundred factors pretty short, relying on what exactly is preserving it down. It need to literally exchange from a 'awful' rating to a 'sincere' one. Which, in turn, means that it may have radical outcomes. It ought to in reality score you better mortgage gives, for starters, further to growth the possibility of you being appeared a hint more favorably in financial establishments and together together with your organisation.

So, what steps do you need to start taking?

Have a Strategic Approach to Paying Your Credit Card

Remember that your credit score rating rating limits and credit score utilization could be very essential as regards to assessing your credit score rating rating. You need to take a look at the rule of the use of much less than 30% on any card, and the decrease that range is, the better. Those who have a totally high credit score rating score will be predisposed to use no more than 7%.

So, you want to test and ensure that your balances are low. If they will be not, surely taking the critical steps to pay down the stableness earlier than the billing cycle ends, or paying a couple of times in some unspecified time in the future of the month to ensure your balance is constantly low.

If you have got got a excessive credit rating usage, then reputation on decreasing the card with the first-rate utilization first, pushing it down till it is 30%, whilst covering the critical hobby and bills of your one-of-a-kind debts till you may get they all under 30%.

Asking For Higher Credit Limits

Now, requesting a higher credit rating restriction does no longer suggest that you could spend more money. Rather, you keep your stability the same, but it straight away starts offevolved to lower your credit rating utilization. This in flip improves your credit rating. So, if you have had a decent pay boom or a touch greater tremendous credit rating experience, then you could have an exquisite danger of getting your self a higher limit.

This may probable seem contradictory, but hold in mind that higher credit score score does not paintings like a loan. It is definitely an business enterprise's permission of the manner an entire lot you are allowed to spend. At the stop of the day, if you make sure you do no longer spend that extra credit score score rating, you're placing your self up for extra achievement. However, in case you do warfare with spending issues, it might be practical to keep away from this step to avoid the possibility of digging yourself right into a more hollow of debt.

Paying Your Bills Right on Time

If you've got were given a reminder set to your cellular telephone, in any other case you installation automatic deposits, then essentially, you could be sure that you can normally make your bills on time. No approach will ever restore your credit score if you hold to pay past due. Late bills may even stay in your credit rating rating rating for over seven years, if now not a hint longer. Generally, if you see which you have not noted a price internal 30 days or greater, you have to call and speak for your creditor at once. Make sure you pay right away or as quickly as you possibly can, and ask if the creditor should endure in thoughts not reporting the left out rate to the credit score bureaus. There isn't any guarantee that the creditor will do that, however you want to be one hundred% exceptional that you pay as rapid as you can and get out of the debt. It is a state of affairs wherein all hands are on deck, and you offer you with a plan. Otherwise, every month which you pass over a rate will deal a blow on your credit score score rating.

How fast will this artwork? This is based upon totally on how many bills you have were given not noted. It furthermore is based upon on how late the charge modified into. The reality is, the greater time that passes after your last overdue rate, the less effect it's going to have inside the eyes of your creditors. However, it'll although have an effect.

So, do whatever you could to ensure you do not bypass over a charge. Do no longer step into any useless contracts or payments, and cancel subscriptions of gadgets you might not be the use of. It is certainly a count number wide variety range of decreasing out the diverse things which could cause a late fee, decreasing the possibilities of detrimental your score.

Dealing With the Collection Accounts

Life can be chaotic and busy, and we may be forgetful. You might have come face-to-face with the reality which you had been mentioned to the debt lenders, and now they are threatening to sue you over your debt. However, after you pay your bills, you might be capable of get the collection organization to save you reporting it.

You can also have those collections out of your report removed inside the occasion that they show symptoms and signs and signs and symptoms of inaccuracy or are too antique to be listed. This, however, can take a incredible quantity of time, and you'll want a strong plan for a way to deal with the collection bills inside the occasion that they appear to be indexed.

Paying Twice a Month

If you've got got had it tough for the final couple months, whether or not or now not it's far converting a window after a golfing ball crashed through it or getting the fan belt on your vehicle changed, this will throw your credit score score utilization thoroughly out of whack, and another time, have an effect to your credit rating. Here is a trick you can examine: Make a call to find out the remaining date (earlier than the credit score score score card company reviews your balance to the credit score bureaus). Then, make payments. Make a charge two weeks earlier than the closing date, and then upload each different rate proper earlier than the final date. This will simplest artwork in case you seem to have the fee range to cowl most, if now not all, of your large charges at the cease of the month.

You really want to keep away from having your credit rating card bring a big bill. You may likely gain more from making use of for a protracted-term loan than attempting it out with the credit score card. Credit playing playing cards aren't built for long time loans.

Being Patient

Patience is honestly not an easy trait to take on whilst watching a totally low credit rating score score. The fact is that you received't be capable of alternate your credit score score rating rating considerably in a single day. The most influential factors that skip into your rating are the commonplace age of facts you have got and the oldest account that is in your report. The problem is that it's far very easy to interrupt an splendid score, and it takes a long term to get over a terrible score. Although restore is without a doubt possible, it may not wholesome into the timeline which you had been hoping for.

Monitoring

You are the protection defend over your very very very own score. Your credit score rating rating requires steady monitoring, and every time you view your very own credit, it's far said that a moderate inquiry has been pulled. This will not have an impact to your private credit rating in the equal manner that difficult inquiries have an impact on your credit.

You will need to test out the fluctuations each few months if you could manipulate it. This will assist you to recognize how properly you're surely handling your credit score rating score and whether or not or not or now not you can provide you with the cash for to take any possibilities or make any changes.

However, all your monetary alternatives will no longer and need to now not hinge genuinely on your credit score score score score. Your credit score want to play an critical characteristic, especially in phrases of picks straight away affecting your credit score score. But if this isn't the case, then you absolutely want to no longer be too pressured about it.

Building a Solid Budget

Bad credit score score ratings are normally created either via surprising instances or terrible making plans. So, having a finances and a plan is likely one of the best strategies to enhance your credit score rating and settle yourself up for enhancing it in the future. You will need to add your credit score rating utilization and calculate truly how a whole lot credit rating you may find the coins for with out falling into deeper debt or exceeding 30% of credit score score utilization.

A strong price range also can show horrific spending conduct, in particular if you preserve consistent and focused song of in which all of your coins goes. Impulse spending is most probable the most crucial responsible birthday celebration in growing credit score score debt.

Budgeting also can provide you with a practical idea of what you could and can't find out the coins for, or even in case your money is truly strained, you could then strategize about which debts and loans to cognizance on and which ones you'll be more lenient with. For instance, the debts which may be at once related in your credit score rating ratings and are therefore likely to be referred to first have to be first in line.

If you truly conflict even with following a price variety, then rope someone you believe in to assist preserve you accountable. It might also seem pointless, but having someone preserve music of your adventure and fulfillment with you will be quite a motivating element.

Ensuring Your Spouse Takes the Same Measures

If you're married, then the credit score record of your partner will also be considered at the same time as you practice for a joint domestic mortgage. You will need to make certain your companion is on the identical course of improvement as you in case you want to enhance your opportunities of having your property loan not unusual.

In this bankruptcy, you decided out that:

You can take greater steps to boost your credit rating score score, together with inquiring for better credit score limits or paying your bills on time.

You want to cope with collection bills right now.

You must usually display your credit score score rating rating carefully.

You want to discover ways to construct a strong rate range.

Healthy Financial Habits to Nurture After Repairing Your Score

Keep up the pleasant artwork, and by no means surrender! The global of budget is filled to the brim with many hints, traps, and times that plenty of us may want to in no way need to see ourselves in, but every now and then, existence can surely push you in.

It is so easy to be tempted with coins, specially in the credit score rating international. When commencing, it is simple to get signed into one debt entice or each other, overspend on one's credit score rating card with money you can't manipulate to pay for to pay decrease once more, and are to be had head to head with lousy behavior that can drag a person's personal credit rating rating into the floor.

Many times, humans don't pretty understand the effect a suffering credit score rating can also have on their lives till they emerge as depending on economic institutions to keep them afloat. It is probably economically hard. It is probably the choice to loosen up and spend money on one's very personal residence, or it may be the choice to excursion the arena, begin a brand new activity, or start a business organization.

People are in big component unprepared for the reality that their credit score score has a massive impact on a number of the selections they would like to make in the future, however you're right here in recent times to begin selecting up accurate behavior. So, allow's recap the whole thing that you have observed.

You now have the fundamental information of FICO and credit score scores, what impact they've got, what they carry about to the table, and the information that they offer. You additionally understand how extended this records want to stay for your report, and what form of human beings will be inclined to paintings together at the side of your credit rating rating file so one can make selections that impact your existence.

Many of the credit score rating score repair corporations exercising the identical recommendations and tips that have been furnished in this ebook, most effective for a rate. However, you can workout the appropriate same tips and achieve the identical consequences. There isn't any intimidating or pushing credit score rating bureaus within the direction which you need. Rather, you'll need to conform to their necessities and tips in case you want to have your rating driven within the proper path.

You have determined out approximately the three most important credit score score bureaus: Equifax, TransUnion, and Experian. You have found out about the rights and responsibilities the credit score rating reporting corporations have in the direction of you due to the fact the creditor and towards institutes and those due to the fact the lenders.

You moreover recognize the way to get proper of get right of entry to in your credit score scores, take a look at your reviews, and get organized in subjects together with expertise your credit score score rating data, paying off crucial debt, writing dispute letters, and studying what exactly can negatively have an effect to your rating.

And with regards to subjects of your credit score score rating, you want to keep away from inaction wherein motion is wanted. Don't exceptional take the essential steps to keep away from the conduct that deliver your credit rating score down, however additionally upload the conduct that shed your monetary facts in a extra exquisite slight.

Chapter 8: What Is A Credit Score?

A credit score rating is a numerical illustration of your creditworthiness and economic health. It is a 3-digit big variety that summarizes your credit rating information and predicts your ability to govern debt responsibly. Lenders, landlords, employers, or maybe coverage groups regularly use credit score scores to assess your monetary trustworthiness.

Importance of Credit Scores:

Understanding the importance of credit score score scores is important for managing your monetary life efficaciously. Here are key reasons why credit rankings count number:

Borrowing Ability: Your credit score rating considerably affects your functionality to borrow money. Whether you are making use of for a mortgage, automobile mortgage, private mortgage, or credit score score card, lenders depend on your credit score score rating to decide whether or not or no longer to approve your software and what terms and interest charges to provide. A immoderate credit rating score can open doorways to better loan alternatives, while a low score also can restrict your alternatives and result in higher borrowing prices.

Interest Rates: When you borrow cash, the interest price you get hold of is right now tied for your credit score rating. A better credit rating score usually ends in lower hobby prices, saving you cash over the lifestyles of a loan. Conversely, a lower score can result in better interest charges, growing the general fee of borrowing.

Renting and Housing: Landlords and assets manipulate groups often test candidates' credit score scores even as locating out whether or now not to rent to them. A strong credit score rating rating can growth your possibilities of securing a apartment belongings, at the same time as a bad score may additionally furthermore reason rejection or require a better protection deposit.

Employment Implications: Some employers bear in mind credit rating facts as a part of their hiring approach, specially for positions regarding economic responsibility. While they can't get proper of access for your credit score score rating, they can evaluate your credit record. A lousy credit record may additionally additionally additionally increase worries about your economic reliability.

Insurance Premiums: Insurance groups can also use credit score score rating-based insurance ratings to determine automobile and home coverage prices. A decrease credit score-based totally insurance score have to result in higher coverage expenses.

Utilities and Services: Utility corporations and provider businesses can also check your credit score whilst you practice for offerings inclusive of mobile smartphone plans, cable TV, or internet subscriptions. A low credit score rating may require a protection deposit or bring about an awful lot an awful lot less favorable phrases.

In precis, your credit score rating rating is a essential monetary device that may impact numerous factors of your lifestyles. Maintaining a wonderful credit score rating score rating can result in more favorable financial possibilities, while a terrible score can present boundaries and boom your standard financial costs. Understanding how credit score rating score rankings artwork and taking steps to control and decorate them is critical for accomplishing your economic desires and securing a sturdy financial future.

How is Your Credit Score Calculated?

Understanding how your credit score score is calculated is critical as it lets in you to take manipulate of your economic behaviors to gain a higher rating. Credit scoring fashions use unique factors to assess your creditworthiness, and each difficulty contains a one-of-a-kind weight in the calculation. Here's a pinnacle degree view of the critical issue factors and their weightage:

1. Payment History (35%):

Factor: Your history of making on-time payments to creditors, along with credit score cards, loans, and mortgages.

Importance: Payment facts is the maximum big element influencing your credit rating score. Consistently paying bills on time is crucial for a excessive credit rating score score.

2. Credit Utilization (30%):

Factor: The quantity of credit score score you are presently the use of in contrast for your total available credit score rating, frequently expressed as a percentage.

Importance: Credit utilization presentations how responsibly you manage your credit rating. Keeping balances low relative in your credit score score rating limits is vital for a brilliant rating.

3. Length of Credit History (15%):

Factor: The time period your credit score score rating debts had been open, which incorporates the age of your oldest and modern day bills, as well as the not unusual age of all money owed.

Importance: A longer credit score rating score statistics can truely impact your score, as it demonstrates your capability to govern credit score through the years.

4. Credit Mix (10%):

Factor: The type of credit score score types you have got, on the facet of credit score rating cards, installment loans (e.G., vehicle loans), and mortgages.

Importance: Having a severa mixture of credit score money owed may be beneficial, however it's far now not as essential as awesome factors.

five. New Credit Inquiries (10%):

Factor: The variety of recent credit inquiries or packages for credit score interior a specific time body.

Importance: Numerous contemporary inquiries can advocate accelerated threat, potentially decreasing your score. Be aware of utilising for credit score score too frequently.

Factors Not Included in Your Credit Score:

Income: Your profits is not a issue in credit score rating scoring models.

Race, Religion, Gender: Credit ratings are not stimulated by using way of personal developments protected beneath anti-discrimination legal guidelines.

Checking Your Own Credit: Checking your personal credit score report (a clean inquiry) does no longer effect your score.

It's critical to be conscious that the particular credit score rating scoring fashions, in conjunction with FICO Score or VantageScore, also can use slightly precise versions of those elements in their calculations. Additionally, the weight of each issue can range, however the opportunities listed proper right here represent a popular guiding precept for maximum credit score rating score scoring fashions.

Improving your credit score rating involves handling the ones factors appropriately. By making nicely timed bills, retaining low credit card balances, maintaining bills open, diversifying your credit combination, and minimizing new credit inquiries, you may take proactive steps to boost your creditworthiness and collect a higher credit rating.

Why Does Your Credit Score Matter?

Your credit score rating score isn't always really some of; it has a vast effect on severa components of your financial lifestyles. Here's why your credit score rating subjects:

1. Impact on Borrowing Ability:

Explanation: Your credit rating rating score plays a pivotal role in figuring out your potential to consistent credit score. Whether you are utilizing for a credit score rating card, automobile mortgage, non-public mortgage, or loan, lenders use your credit rating score to assess your creditworthiness.

Importance: A better credit score rating rating rating will growth your chances of loan approval. It also can increase your borrowing alternatives and can help you get admission to loans with extra favorable phrases, together with lower interest prices and better credit score score rating limits. Conversely, a low credit score may also additionally moreover restriction your borrowing alternatives and bring about a good deal much less favorable mortgage terms or even loan rejection.

2. Influence on Interest Rates:

Explanation: When you borrow cash, the hobby fee you get maintain of is right away linked for your credit score score score. Lenders offer decrease hobby prices to people with better credit rating score rankings due to the fact they will be perceived as decrease credit rating score dangers.

Importance: A better credit rating score rating can save you lots of dollars in interest payments over the existence of a loan. Lower hobby charges recommend you pay a lot much much less for the cash you borrow, which permit you to obtain your economic dreams extra efficaciously.

three. Role in Renting and Housing:

Explanation: Landlords and belongings manage agencies often use credit score rankings to evaluate rental candidates. A well credit score can improve your possibilities of renting a favored condominium or residence. Conversely, a low score can also lead to rejection or require a larger safety deposit.

Importance: A sturdy credit rating can offer you with greater housing options and possibly prevent coins with the aid of avoiding better safety deposits.

four. Employment Implications:

Explanation: Some employers may also moreover evaluation credit score score rating reviews as a part of their hiring way, specifically for positions regarding monetary responsibility. While they can't get entry to your credit rating score, a awful credit score file also can enhance issues approximately your monetary reliability.

Importance: A terrible credit score information have to impact your employability, in all likelihood limiting your assignment possibilities. Maintaining an superb credit score rating is important for profession improvement in positive industries.

In precis, your credit score score rating is a important monetary tool that affects your ability to get proper of get admission to to credit score, the fee of borrowing, housing options, or even employment opportunities. A robust credit rating can open doorways to monetary possibilities and offer you with extra favorable phrases, on the same time as a low score may also additionally cause barriers and higher fees. Recognizing the importance of your credit score score empowers you to take control of your financial future and make informed picks to improve and hold your creditworthiness.

Chapter 9: Credit Reports

Your credit score score record is an in depth document of your monetary statistics and credit score rating score-related sports. Understanding it's miles crucial for handling your credit score rating efficaciously. This section will manual you on a manner to gain, evaluate, and interpret your credit score report, further to a way to dispute mistakes:

1. How to Obtain Your Credit Report:

Obtaining Your Free Annual Credit Report: Federal law allows you to advantage one free credit file each year from every of the 3 fundamental credit score score bureaus: Equifax, Experian, and TransUnion. To get right of entry to your unfastened annual evaluations, go to AnnualCreditReport.Com, the exceptional criminal internet web page for this reason.

Additional Reports: In addition on your unfastened annual evaluations, you can request your credit score record in case you've been denied credit score, employment, or insurance based totally mostly on your credit score score statistics. You may additionally additionally request a report in case you suspect identity theft or fraud.

2. Reviewing and Interpreting Your Credit Report:

Checking Personal Information: Start with the aid of manner of reviewing your personal facts, at the facet of your call, address, Social Security range, and employment statistics. Ensure that each one information are correct and updated.

Account Information: Examine the listing of your credit score money owed, together with credit score score gambling playing playing cards, loans, and mortgages. Verify that every account is yours and that the account statuses are accurate (e.G., open, closed, or in right reputation).

Payment History: Assess your charge records for each credit score account. It need to mirror whether or not you've got made payments on time, had any overdue bills, or skilled delinquencies.

Credit Inquiries: Take phrase of inquiries to your credit file. Hard inquiries occur while you observe for credit, whilst smooth inquiries (now not affecting your score) frequently end result from ancient past checks or your own credit score checks.

Public Records: Check for any horrific public records, which encompass bankruptcies, tax liens, or civil judgments. These can appreciably impact your credit score rating.

Collection Accounts: Identify any money owed which have been despatched to collections. These debts have a damaging impact to your credit score rating.

Credit Scores: Some credit rating reviews provide your credit rating rating. However, you could want to get admission to your score one by one through credit score rating monitoring services.

three. Disputing Errors on Your Report:

Identifying Errors: If you see inaccuracies or discrepancies on your credit record, which include wrong account records, rate mistakes, or unexpected bills, it is important to accomplish that.

Initiating Disputes: To dispute mistakes, contact the credit bureau reporting the wrong facts. You can typically provoke disputes on line, by means of using way of mail, or over the cellular telephone. Be organized to provide documentation assisting your dispute.

Investigation Process: After receiving your dispute, the credit score bureau will look at the trouble and art work with the furnisher of the records (e.G., a creditor) to verify the accuracy of the records.

Resolution: The credit bureau will inform you of the consequences of the studies. If the disputed information is found to be erroneous, it's far going to be corrected or eliminated from your credit score rating score report.

Regularly reviewing your credit score report guarantees its accuracy and enables you become aware of and deal with problems directly. Disputing mistakes is crucial for maintaining a wholesome credit score rating profile and ensuring that your credit rating score as it need to be displays your creditworthiness.

Types of Credit Scores

Credit ratings aren't one-length-fits-all; there are numerous scoring fashions used by lenders and economic institutions. In this segment, we'll discover the 2 number one credit rating rating scoring fashions, FICO Score and VantageScore, similarly to company-specific scores:

1. FICO Score vs. VantageScore:

FICO Score: The FICO Score is one of the maximum widely diagnosed and used credit score rating scoring fashions. It become evolved thru the Fair Isaac Corporation (FICO) and has severa variations tailor-made to unique sorts of lending, collectively with FICO Auto Score for vehicle loans and FICO Mortgage Score for mortgages. FICO Scores generally variety from 3 hundred to 850, with higher rankings indicating higher creditworthiness.

VantageScore: VantageScore is each different fundamental credit score rating score scoring version created through manner of the three critical credit score score bureaus: Equifax, Experian, and TransUnion. VantageScores moreover range from three hundred to 850 and are used by many lenders. VantageScore has its private variations designed for one-of-a-kind lending features, alongside aspect VantageScore Auto for car loans and VantageScore three.Zero for extremely-cutting-edge credit score score evaluation.

Key Differences: While each FICO Score and VantageScore study creditworthiness, they may use slightly wonderful algorithms and weight factors. As a forestall end result, your rating may also moreover range barely the various 2 fashions. It's critical to expose every your FICO Score and VantageScore to have a comprehensive statistics of your credit score score fitness.

2. Industry-Specific Scores:

Auto Credit Scores: Lenders inside the car corporation can also use specialized credit score ratings tailored to assess a borrower's chance of repaying an car loan. These scores do not forget elements unique to vehicle financing, such as your data of automobile loan payments and the varieties of cars you've got financed.

Mortgage Credit Scores: Mortgage lenders often use credit rating rankings designed mainly for loan lending choices. These scores bear in thoughts your mortgage rate facts and the way you have got controlled past mortgages.

Credit Card Scores: Credit card issuers might also rent proprietary scoring fashions to assess your eligibility for his or her credit card merchandise. These rankings prioritize factors associated with credit score card usage, such as your credit score rating rating card charge data and usage price.

Understanding which credit score scores are applicable on your economic dreams is vital. Different lenders and industries may additionally depend upon unique scoring fashions to assess credit score candidates. To hold appropriate credit rating fitness, often show your credit rating rankings from a couple of belongings and address any discrepancies or mistakes immediately. This proactive technique ensures that you're nicely-organized even as searching out credit score rating score for numerous purposes, from purchasing for a automobile to securing a mortgage.

What Makes a Good Credit Score?

Understanding what constitutes an extraordinary credit score rating rating is critical for dealing with your financial fitness and accomplishing your monetary dreams. In this segment, we are able to discover credit rating degrees and the way lenders apprehend particular rating degrees:

1. Credit Score Ranges:

Excellent (750-850): Credit ratings on this variety are taken into consideration extraordinary. Individuals with scores on the better end of this variety commonly have a history of usually making on-time bills, preserving low credit score card balances, and coping with severa varieties of credit rating responsibly. They revel in access to the pleasant lending phrases and hobby prices.

Good (700-749): Good credit score score ratings mean responsible credit score rating control. Borrowers with ratings on this variety are normally seemed favorably through creditors. They are likely to qualify for max loans and credit score rating gambling cards at aggressive charges.

Fair (650-699): Scores in the sincere range may recommend a few credit demanding situations or occasional past due payments. Borrowers with honest credit score score may additionally however qualify for loans and credit score gambling gambling playing cards, however they will come upon higher interest charges and masses less favorable terms.

Poor (550-649): Credit ratings within the terrible range may also sign a records of exceptional credit score issues, along side delinquencies, collections, or excessive credit score card balances. Borrowers in this class may locate it greater tough to strong credit rating score, and if criminal, they may face excessive interest fees and stringent terms.

Very Poor (3 hundred-549): Very awful credit scores indicate immoderate credit score rating worrying situations, together with a couple of past due bills, charge-offs, and potentially bankruptcies. Borrowers with very horrific credit score score score may additionally moreover have restrained get right of access to to credit score rating alternatives and face excessive interest prices and unfavorable terms.

2. How Lenders Perceive Different Score Levels:

Excellent and Good Scores: Lenders generally view debtors with first rate and accurate credit score rankings as low-threat. These borrowers are more likely to be set up for loans and credit score score rating playing cards with favorable hobby costs and terms. Lenders trust in their potential to repay debt responsibly.

Fair Scores: Borrowers with honest credit rating rankings may additionally additionally despite the fact that be famous for credit, but lenders may also workout caution. They may offer credit score score at barely higher hobby prices or with stricter terms to mitigate potential chance.

Poor and Very Poor Scores: Individuals with terrible or very horrible credit score scores can also face full-size stressful conditions even as looking for credit score score. Lenders can be extra selective, and if frequent, borrowers might also additionally come upon immoderate hobby expenses and large charges because of the perceived better threat.

It's crucial to study that on the same time as credit score rating rating ratings play a essential feature in lending picks, lenders furthermore consider different elements, in conjunction with profits, employment stability, and the particular mortgage or credit score card product being implemented for. Additionally, specific creditors may additionally additionally moreover have varying criteria and chance tolerance ranges.

To keep or improve your credit score score score, reputation on accountable credit score score control practices, collectively with making on-time bills, retaining credit score card balances low, and monitoring your credit score score record for accuracy. A suitable credit score rating score no longer best opens doorways to credit score rating possibilities but additionally contributes in your simple monetary nicely-being.

Chapter 10: How to Improve Your Credit Score

Improving your credit score score rating is an crucial a part of handling your financial fitness and securing favorable lending terms. Here are key strategies to help beautify your credit score score score:

1. Establishing a Credit History:

Apply for a Credit Card: If you do not have a credit rating score facts, keep in mind utilising for a secured credit rating score card or turning into a licensed user on a person else's credit card. Responsible use of these playing gambling playing cards can help installation a first-rate credit score facts.

Student Loans or Credit Builder Loans: If you are a student or have restricted credit score score, pupil loans or credit score builder loans are options to begin constructing credit rating.

2. Managing Credit Utilization:

Maintain Low Balances: Keep your credit score card balances low in phrases of your credit score limits. High credit score rating card balances can negatively impact your credit score score rating.

Pay Down Debt: Reducing gift credit score card balances may moreover have a large terrific impact for your credit score score score. Aim to pay down immoderate-interest money owed first.

3. Paying Bills on Time:

On-Time Payments: Consistently pay your payments on time, as price information is a vital detail to your credit score score. Late payments can have a long-lasting horrific effect.

Set Up Payment Reminders: Use reminders or automatic payments to make certain you by no means omit a due date.

4. Handling Existing Debt:

Create a Repayment Plan: If you have got significant debt, enlarge a based compensation plan. Paying down debt demonstrates accountable economic control and can beautify your credit score score score through the years.

Avoid Closing Old Accounts: Closing vintage credit score rating card debts can shorten your credit score rating information, potentially decreasing your rating. Keep older payments open and use them sometimes to keep interest.

five. Avoiding Common Credit Mistakes:

Don't Apply for Too Much Credit: Each credit rating software program commonly consequences in a tough inquiry, that may in short lower your score. Avoid utilising for more than one credit playing playing playing cards or loans in a quick period.

Monitor Your Credit Report: Regularly assessment your credit report for mistakes or inaccuracies. Dispute any discrepancies with the credit score rating bureaus.

Be Cautious with Retail Store Cards: Retail maintain credit score rating playing playing cards frequently have excessive interest prices and can encourage impulsive spending. Use them judiciously.

6. Gradually Build Credit Mix:

Diversify Credit Types: Over time, take into account diversifying your credit combo. Having a aggregate of credit rating sorts, at the side of credit score rating playing gambling playing cards, installment loans, and mortgages, can in reality impact your rating.

7. Seek Professional Help When Needed:

Credit Counseling: If you are struggling with debt and credit control, do not forget seeking out credit score counseling from a reputable employer. They can offer steering on debt reimbursement and budgeting.

Remember that enhancing your credit rating score rating is a slow machine, and there are no quick fixes. Be affected character and stay committed to responsible financial habits. Your credit rating score score suggests your creditworthiness, and immoderate fine changes can lead to higher lending terms, decrease interest costs, and accelerated economic opportunities in the destiny.

Tips for Building and Rebuilding Credit

Whether you are beginning from scratch or running to rebuild your credit score, there are various powerful strategies that will help you set up or enhance your creditworthiness:

1. Secured Credit Cards:

How They Work: Secured credit score score rating gambling gambling playing cards require a protection deposit, which commonly becomes your credit limit. These cards are an amazing option for people and no longer using a credit score rating records or horrific credit score.

Responsible Use: Make small, achievable purchases and usually pay your secured card balance on time. Over time, responsible use can cause an progressed credit score score score.

Transition to Unsecured: Some secured card issuers provide the possibility to transition to an unsecured card after demonstrating responsible credit score conduct.

2. Credit-Builder Loans:

Purpose: Credit-builder loans are designed that will help you gather credit score gradually. They art work by means of the usage of manner of having you are making small, regular bills into a financial monetary savings account. Once the mortgage term is whole, you obtain the charge variety, and your on-time payments are cited to the credit rating bureaus.

Payment Consistency: Timely payments on a credit score-builder loan can certainly impact your credit score rating rating and set up a nice fee statistics.

3. Authorized User Status:

Joining Someone Else's Account: You can ask a member of the family or buddy to feature you as a licensed character on their credit rating card account. This lets in you to benefit from their terrific rate information and age of the account.

Caution: Ensure that the number one account holder has a records of accountable credit rating control, as any horrible movements at the account can also affect your credit score.

four. Reporting Rent and Utility Payments:

Alternative Data Reporting: Some credit bureaus and offerings permit you to have your rent and software application payments said to your credit report as non-conventional credit rating information. This can help beautify your credit rating rating via using showcasing your responsible fee history.

Ask Your Landlord or Utility Provider: Inquire if your landlord or software program company offers this reporting provider, and if now not, discover zero.33-birthday party offerings that could help.

five. Maintain Low Credit Card Balances:

Credit Utilization: Keep your credit score rating score card balances low in phrases of your credit score limits. High credit score rating card balances can negatively effect your credit score rating score.

Pay in Full: Whenever feasible, goal to pay your credit score rating rating card balances in complete each month to avoid interest fees.

6. Timely Payments: The most vital trouble in constructing and maintaining actual credit score score is constantly making on-time payments for all of your credit score score rating responsibilities, collectively with loans, credit score score gambling playing playing cards, and payments.

7. Monitor Your Progress: Regularly test your credit score rating document to music your credit score rating-building development and make certain there are not any mistakes or discrepancies.

eight. Avoid New Credit Applications: Limit new credit applications, especially if you're strolling to rebuild credit score rating score. Each application can bring about a hard inquiry, which can also additionally in brief decrease your rating.

9. Patience and Persistence: Building or rebuilding credit rating takes time, so be affected person and chronic for your efforts. Continue running towards accountable credit rating conduct, and your score will frequently beautify.

Remember that constructing or rebuilding credit score score is a journey, and there are not any shortcuts. Consistency in responsible credit score manipulate is prime to accomplishing and maintaining a wholesome credit rating score, that could open doors to better monetary possibilities.

Credit Repair vs. Credit Improvement

Understanding the difference amongst credit score restore and credit rating improvement is critical for dealing with your credit correctly. In this section, we are able to find out the versions a number of the two and while it is able to be suitable to keep in mind credit score rating repair offerings:

1. The Difference Between Repairing and Improving Credit:

Credit Repair: Credit restore includes the way of addressing and rectifying mistakes, inaccuracies, or bad objects to your credit score score report. The primary aim is to remove or accurate those gadgets to decorate your credit score. Common troubles addressed in credit rating repair consist of past due payments, collections, price-offs, and other horrible marks.

Credit Improvement: Credit development, rather, specializes in adopting accountable credit rating control conduct to enhance your creditworthiness over time. This approach consists of making properly timed bills, reducing credit rating card balances, and preserving a top notch price records.

2. When to Consider Credit Repair Services:

Errors on Your Credit Report: If you take into account there are mistakes or inaccuracies to your credit document that are negatively impacting your credit score score, you can remember credit score restore offerings. Common errors embody wrong account information, debts that do not belong to you, and old or replica entries.

Negative Items that Can Be Challenged: Some terrible gadgets on your credit score file can be legally challengeable, which incorporates gadgets which may be inaccurately noted or beyond the statute of obstacles. Credit repair specialists permit you to navigate the dispute device and advocate on your behalf.

Lack of Time or Expertise: If you're beaten via the credit score rating repair method or lack the realise-a way to correctly dispute errors, credit score score repair offerings can be a treasured resource. These experts have enjoy in navigating credit rating reporting businesses' methods and guidelines.

Important Considerations:

DIY Credit Repair: It's possible to adopt credit score restore for your personal with the useful resource of reviewing your credit score opinions, figuring out mistakes, and disputing inaccuracies. You have the right to dispute records with the credit score rating rating bureaus for gratis.

Credit Repair Services: When choosing a credit score repair enterprise organization, be cautious and do your studies. Look for professional companies with a data of success, obvious pricing, and a clean understanding of the Credit Repair Organizations Act (CROA), which regulates the enterprise.

Credit Improvement: While credit repair can address particular troubles in your credit file, ongoing credit score rating improvement consists of accountable economic behavior. Regularly paying payments on time, coping with credit score score score card balances, and maintaining off new credit inquiries all make a contribution to credit score development.

Credit Counseling: If you're struggling with overwhelming debt, credit score rating counseling agencies can provide guidance on debt control and budgeting, that may motive every credit rating restore and credit score score improvement.

It's crucial to method credit score restore and credit score development with sensible expectancies. Credit repair can also result in the elimination of inaccuracies, but it is able to now not dramatically change your credit score if the horrible statistics is correct. Ultimately, building and preserving specific credit is based on responsible credit score control practices through the years.

Chapter 11: Maintaining a Good Credit Score

Once you have got were given carried out a first rate credit rating score or correctly advanced your credit rating rating, it's far vital to keep that powerful creditworthiness through the years. In this phase, we are going to discover key practices for preserving an high-quality credit rating:

1. Consistency in Financial Habits:

Timely Payments: Continue making all your bills on time, collectively with credit rating card payments, mortgage payments, and utility payments. Consistently paying payments by their due dates is one of the maximum important factors in preserving a awesome credit score rating rating.

Responsible Credit Card Use: Keep your credit card balances low in assessment to your credit score rating score limits. Avoid wearing excessive balances, as excessive credit score card debt can negatively impact your credit score rating rating score. Aim to pay your

144

credit score card balances in entire each month on every occasion feasible.

2. Regularly Monitoring Your Credit:

Review Your Credit Reports: Regularly take a look at your credit score reviews from all three vital credit rating bureaus—Equifax, Experian, and TransUnion. You're entitled to 1 loose document from each bureau annually thru AnnualCreditReport.Com. Reviewing your opinions allows you to encounter any errors, inaccuracies, or signs and symptoms and signs and symptoms and signs and symptoms of identity robbery.

Consider Credit Monitoring Services: If you want ongoing get admission to on your credit score reports and rankings, you can be part of credit score score tracking offerings. These services offer actual-time credit rating tracking, indicators for wonderful changes, and credit score score rating updates.

3. Safeguarding Your Personal Information:

Protect Your Personal Data: Guard your personal facts, which incorporates your Social Security wide range, monetary account numbers, and sensitive login credentials. Avoid sharing touchy statistics over unsecured channels or with unverified human beings.

Be Cautious Online: Use robust and precise passwords on your economic debts. Be cautious at the same time as presenting personal statistics online and confirm the legitimacy of web sites and electronic mail communications.

Monitor for Identity Theft: Regularly have a look at your financial statements and payments for unauthorized transactions. If you trust you studied identification robbery or fraudulent hobby, take instantaneous motion to report and solve it.

4. Avoid Unnecessary Credit Inquiries:

Minimize New Credit Applications: Limit the range of latest credit score rating card or loan programs you placed up, specifically inside a brief time frame. Each credit score score inquiry can bring about a short dip in your credit score rating.

five. Keep Older Accounts Open:

Maintain Credit History: Older credit rating debts make a contribution positively for your credit score score through growing the not unusual age of your credit rating rating facts. Avoid last vintage payments, even in case you do no longer often use them.

6. Responsible Debt Management:

Manage Debt Wisely: If you have were given loans or credit score rating rating card debt, focus on coping with it responsibly. Make consistent payments and keep away from amassing immoderate new debt.

Plan for Life Changes: Consider how widespread existence sports, which encompass a challenge alternate or relocation, can effect your credit rating. Be prepared to adapt your monetary strategies therefore.

7. Seek Professional Guidance When Necessary:

Credit Counseling: If you come across monetary challenges, such as overwhelming debt, recall looking for assist from a credit score counseling employer. They will permit you to create a debt management plan and offer treasured economic steering.

Maintaining a superb credit score score score score is an ongoing self-control to responsible financial behavior and vigilance in competition to capacity threats in your credit rating. By continuously schooling those credit score score rating-savvy behaviors, you may make sure that your credit stays in exquisite popularity and keeps to benefit your monetary dreams and possibilities.

Credit Score Myths and Facts

Credit ratings are an essential trouble of private finance, however there are numerous myths and misconceptions surrounding them. In this segment, we're going to debunk some common credit score rating score myths and offer the facts:

Myth 1: Checking Your Own Credit Hurts Your Score.

Fact: Checking your very very very own credit rating score, referred to as a soft inquiry or gentle pull, does no longer effect your credit rating. It's considered a accountable economic exercise to expose your credit score score frequently.

Myth 2: Closing Old Credit Card Accounts Boosts Your Score.

Fact: Closing older credit card money owed can actually lower your credit rating. Older payments make a contribution honestly for your credit rating rating information's not unusual age. Keeping them open can benefit your rating.

Myth 3: Paying Off a Negative Debt Removes It from Your Report.

Fact: Paying off a debt that has lengthy past to collections or changed into charged off is a fantastic step, however it would not mechanically remove the poor get admission to from your credit file. It will though be listed, but as "Paid."

Myth four: You Have Only One Credit Score.

Fact: You have a couple of credit rating rankings, no longer simply one. Various scoring fashions, like FICO and VantageScore, are utilized by creditors, and each may also moreover produce a barely truly considered one of a kind score.

Myth 5: Income Affects Your Credit Score.

Fact: Your earnings isn't always a right away element on your credit score score rating calculation. Lenders undergo in mind your earnings while comparing your potential to repay a mortgage, but it is no longer part of your credit score rating rating rating.

Myth 6: You Need to Carry a Balance on Your Credit Card to Build Credit.

Fact: Carrying a balance is not essential for building credit score score score. You can construct credit score through manner of creating small, ordinary fees for your credit rating rating card and paying the stability in entire each month.

Myth 7: Your Marital Status Affects Your Credit Score.

Fact: Your marital recognition does now not effect your credit score rating rating. Credit reviews and rankings are person, not joint, besides you've got a joint account.

Myth eight: Co-Signing Doesn't Affect Your Credit.

Fact: Co-signing for a loan or credit score card makes you in addition accountable for the debt, and it seems in your credit score report. Late bills or defaults through the number one borrower can damage your credit score.

Myth nine: Bad Credit Lasts Forever.

Fact: Negative records normally remains on your credit rating record for a fantastic length, which incorporates seven years for maximum sorts of terrible objects. With accountable credit score score management, you could rebuild your credit over the years.

Myth 10: You Can Quickly Repair Bad Credit.

Fact: Credit restore takes time, and there aren't any immediate fixes. Improving your credit score rating consists of constant, accountable monetary behavior and addressing inaccuracies on your credit file.

Myth eleven: Paying Off Collections Removes Them from Your Report.

Fact: Paying off collections debts may additionally moreover improve your score, however the get admission to will despite the fact that be in your document, generally marked as "Paid." It might not actually do away with the statistics.

Understanding the ones credit score score rating myths and information is critical for making knowledgeable economic alternatives and averting commonplace misconceptions that would impact your credit score control. Always are looking for reliable property of records in terms of understanding and improving your credit rating.

Credit Score and Your Financial Goals

Your credit score score plays a large function in accomplishing your financial goals and aspirations. In this section, we are going to discover how a extremely good credit score score score allow you to reach particular economic goals and the importance of the use of credit rating strategically:

1. Achieving Specific Financial Objectives:

Homeownership: A pinnacle credit score rating score rating is frequently critical at the identical time as making use of for a mortgage to shop for a home. Lenders use your credit score rating to evaluate your creditworthiness and decide your eligibility for a loan mortgage. A better credit score score can bring about higher hobby charges and extra favorable mortgage terms, in all likelihood saving you masses of dollars over the life of your mortgage.

Vehicle Financing: When buying a car, your credit rating rating may have an impact at the hobby rate on your vehicle loan. A proper credit score rating score also can qualify you for lower fees, decreasing the overall fee of the car and making your monthly payments more potential.

Credit Card Rewards: Many credit score card issuers offer rewards, cashback, or travel factors to cardholders with relevant credit score rating. With a higher credit score, you can get entry to credit playing playing cards that offer appealing rewards, assisting you keep cash on everyday costs or tour.

Small Business Financing: If you are an entrepreneur or small organization owner, your personal credit rating score may be evaluated when searching for agency financing. A right private credit score score

score can beautify your chances of securing corporation loans or traces of credit score score to fund your ventures.

2. Using Credit Strategically:

Credit Building: A genuine credit rating score isn't pretty masses getting accepted for loans; it is also about using credit strategically to assemble a robust credit score rating score records. Responsible credit card use, well timed bills, and keeping low credit score card balances make a contribution to a top notch credit score rating profile.

Emergency Fund: While credit score score score may be a financial safety internet ultimately of emergencies, it's far crucial to have an emergency fund as your first line of safety. An emergency fund will let you cowl sudden costs without relying mostly on credit score playing playing playing cards or loans.

Avoiding High-Interest Debt: Good credit score offers get admission to to loans with lower hobby prices. However, it is crucial to keep away from accumulating high-interest debt, as hobby prices can speedy erode your financial improvement. Paying off credit score score card balances in whole each month minimizes hobby expenses.

Credit Card Utilization: Keep your credit score card balances properly under your credit score limits to hold a healthy credit rating rating utilization ratio. This demonstrates responsible credit manipulate to lenders and may surely effect your credit score rating.

Credit Monitoring: Regularly display your credit score reviews and ratings to stay informed about your credit score fitness. Early detection of errors or symptoms and symptoms and signs of identity theft will can help you take spark off motion to rectify troubles.

3. Long-Term Financial Stability:

A suitable credit score score score rating isn't pretty a lot right now financial desires; it is an critical element of your prolonged-term monetary balance. It can open doors to higher economic opportunities, which includes decrease interest expenses on loans, extended get right of entry to to credit score, and favorable insurance prices. By keeping proper credit score score, you characteristic your self for a stronger and extra strong monetary future.

Remember that while a outstanding credit rating rating may be a precious tool, it's important to apply credit score rating responsibly and within your approach. Achieving financial desires goes hand in hand with prudent financial control, which includes budgeting, saving, and making an investment wisely. By combining a strong credit score score with sound financial conduct, you can pave the way to a wealthy economic future.

Chapter 12: Assessing Your Current Credit Situation

Understanding your cutting-edge-day credit score rating scenario is the vital first step on your credit score restore journey. In this economic smash, we will discover a manner to gain your credit score score record, why it's far essential to study it for accuracy, and a way to perceive horrible devices which may be affecting your credit rating.

Section 2.1: Obtaining Your Credit Report

To begin, you can want to gain a reproduction of your credit rating score record. Under federal regulation, you are entitled to at the least one loose credit score score document every three hundred and sixty 5 days from every of the 3 critical credit score score reporting businesses:

Here are the important issue steps to gain your credit score rating rating document:

1. Visit AnnualCreditReport.

2. Request your credit score rating record from one of the 3 critical groups.

three. Verify your identification by providing personal records.

4. Choose which report(s) you want, as you could stagger your requests over the 3 hundred and sixty 5 days to show your credit score score extra regularly.

Section 2.2: Reviewing Your Credit Report for Accuracy

Once you've got were given your credit rating document in hand, it is time to check it closely. Pay attention to the subsequent records:

1. Personal Information: Ensure your call, address, and exceptional non-public records are accurate. Mistakes on this phase can now and again be a hallmark of identification theft.

2. Account Information: Examine every account listed, together with credit score rating playing gambling cards, loans, and

mortgages. Check for inaccuracies in account balances, rate records, and account reputation.

3. Public Records: Look for any bankruptcies, tax liens, or civil judgments indexed. These bad gadgets can significantly impact your credit rating rating.

4. Credit Inquiries: Review the list of inquiries made into your credit score rating report. Authorized inquiries from creditors are regular, however too many inquiries in a short duration also can negatively have an impact on your score.

5. Collections: Verify if any debts had been sent to collections. These can be mainly poor in your credit score rating.

Section 2.Three: Identifying Negative Items Affecting Your Credit Score

Negative objects for your credit score report, collectively with overdue payments, charge-offs, or collections, could have a outstanding horrible effect in your credit score score.

Make a notice of any of these devices as you assessment your document. These are areas you will want to address on your credit score score score repair plan.

It's vital to dispute any inaccuracies you find out to your credit record. If you discover errors, you could report a dispute with the credit score rating reporting businesses to have them corrected. Be organized to provide documentation to help your dispute.

Remember, the accuracy of your credit file is paramount, and correcting errors can drastically beautify your credit score. In the subsequent chapters, we are going to delve into strategies for addressing and resolving terrible devices to your record and developing a complete credit score rating repair plan tailor-made on your precise dreams. By taking the ones steps, you'll be properly on your manner to improving your credit and carrying out your financial desires.

Setting Your Credit Repair Goals

Before diving into the nitty-gritty of repairing your credit, it is important to set smooth and practicable goals. Your credit score score rating repair journey ought to be realistic and centered to make the maximum considerable effect to your economic well-being. In this financial catastrophe, we're going to discover the way to set your credit rating score restore dreams, every quick-time period and lengthy-time period, and installation a realistic timeline to guide your development.

Section 3.1: Why Setting Credit Repair Goals Matters

Setting desires provides you with a roadmap in your credit score rating score repair journey. It enables you stay targeted, brought about, and responsible. Whether you are looking to shop for a home, constant a higher hobby price on a loan, or certainly beautify your monetary standing, easy dreams will guide your actions.

Section 3.2: Establishing Clear Objectives

Begin with the aid of manner of the use of figuring out what you purpose to attain thru credit score score repair. Common goals may additionally include:

1. Credit Score Improvement: Set a particular goal for your credit rating score score. For example, increasing your FICO rating from six hundred to seven-hundred.

2. Debt Reduction: Reducing your splendid debt with the beneficial aid of a selected quantity or percent.

three. Qualifying for a Loan: Preparing your credit to solid a loan, vehicle loan, or private loan.

four. Lowering Interest Rates: Qualifying for lower interest costs on present loans and credit score score rating playing cards.

five. Financial Stability: Establishing a credit rating basis for future economic balance.

Section three.Three: Short-Term and Long-Term Goals

It's vital to set every brief-term and prolonged-time period goals. Short-term goals must be possible inner a few months, at the same time as extended-time period dreams may also furthermore span severa years. This dual technique ensures you have got amusing small victories alongside the way and keep motivation for the larger image.

Short-time period desires might encompass:

Disputing and casting off errors from your credit score document.

Paying off one or more small debts. Reducing credit card balances.

Long-time period dreams may additionally moreover need to embody:

Achieving a specific credit rating score interior a 12 months or .

Saving for a down price on a home.

Qualifying for a specific mortgage or credit score score card with favorable phrases.

Section 3.Four: Creating a Realistic Timeline

Developing a timeline is vital for tracking your development. Consider elements which includes your cutting-edge credit rating score, the severity of horrible devices, and your economic property. Be sensible about how much time it is able to take to reap your desires. Setting an aggressive timeline can bring about frustration, at the equal time as a totally conservative one would possibly likely stall your development.

A realistic timeline may also embody:

Reviewing and disputing credit score document errors within the first month.

Creating a charge range and debt reduce charge plan interior months.

Consistently making on-time payments for at least six months.

Gradually developing your credit score rating score rating over the path of a one year or more.

Section 3.5: Regularly Review and Adjust Your Goals

As you development in your credit score score restore journey, periodically examine and modify your dreams. You might also additionally attain a few goals greater rapid than predicted, at the same time as others may additionally additionally take longer. Flexibility is top. Reassessing your dreams guarantees you stay heading within the proper path and preserve to make knowledgeable picks approximately your credit score rating restore approach.

By setting clear, doable credit rating restore desires, you could have a roadmap to guide your moves and measure your fulfillment. In the following chapters, we're going to delve into the practical steps to create a credit repair plan that aligns in conjunction with your objectives. Your dreams might be the using stress inside the back of your determination to enhancing your credit score rating and engaging in your financial goals.

Chapter 13: Creating a Credit Repair Plan

In the preceding chapters, you have received an expertise of credit score score rankings, assessed your credit rating record, and set easy credit score rating repair desires. Now, it's time to growth an entire credit score rating restore plan to help you gather the ones goals. This bankruptcy will manual you via the technique of making a customized movement plan to deal with the horrible items for your credit record and ultimately enhance your credit score score score.

Section 4.1: Prioritizing Negative Items

Begin by using categorizing the terrible gadgets for your credit score score file into tremendous priority tiers. Not all horrible items have the same impact in your credit score rating, so it is important to pick out out the maximum vital ones to deal with first. Priority degrees would possibly embody:

1. High Priority: Items with the maximum large terrible effect, collectively with overdue payments or collections.

2. Medium Priority: Negative gadgets which might be moderately unfavorable, like rate-offs or older past due payments.

three. Low Priority: Items with a especially minor effect, together with a single not noted charge from numerous years within the past.

Section four.2: Creating a Dispute Strategy

For excessive and medium priority devices, you will want to dispute inaccuracies with the credit score rating reporting organizations. Develop a technique for each dispute, which includes:

1. Gather Evidence: Collect documentation that lets in your dispute, collectively with price records, correspondence, or proof of inaccuracies.

2. Write Effective Dispute Letters: Craft properly-based dispute letters that actually define the errors and request correction. Be high-quality to ship those letters through licensed mail to maintain a file of conversation.

three. Follow-Up: Track the development of your disputes and take a look at up with the credit reporting agencies if important. They have 30 days to analyze and reply to your dispute.

Section four.Three: Debt Reduction and Payment Plans

For items that are not because of errors however are affecting your credit rating score, which encompass excessive credit score score card balances, create a debt bargain plan. This could possibly contain:

1. Budgeting: Establish a budget to govern your month-to-month costs and allocate fee range for debt compensation.

2. Negotiation: Contact lenders to barter settlements, charge plans, or hobby fee reductions if applicable.

3. Consistent Payments: Commit to creating on-time bills to all of your lenders and lenders, as charge information significantly affects your credit score rating.

Section 4.Four: Building Positive Credit

Simultaneously, paintings on constructing tremendous credit. Positive credit score score statistics can offset the impact of bad gadgets and help enhance your credit rating rating score over time. Consider the following techniques:

1. Secured Credit Cards: Apply for a secured credit score rating score card to illustrate responsible credit score utilization.

2. Credit Builder Loans: Explore credit score rating builder loans, particularly designed to assist humans set up or rebuild credit score.

three. Authorized User: Become a licensed consumer on a family member or friend's credit score rating card with a remarkable charge records.

four. Good Credit Habits: Maintain fantastic credit score conduct by means of paying payments on time, now not maxing out credit score playing cards, and handling credit responsibly.

170

Section four.Five: Monitoring Your Progress

Consistently tracking your credit score score is important to music your progress and discover any discrepancies or new terrible objects which can seem. You can use on-line credit rating tracking services or the unfastened annual credit score score reviews to keep a close to eye in your credit score rating score records.

Remember that credit rating repair isn't always a quick recuperation, but rather a journey that requires strength of mind and patience. Your credit rating rating repair plan must be adaptable and evolve as you gain milestones and come across new worrying conditions. In the approaching chapters, we are able to find out particular strategies for dealing with credit score rating record mistakes, coping with debt, and building excessive extremely good credit. With a properly-structured plan in area, you're in your manner to engaging in your credit score

score restore goals and taking manipulate of your economic future.

Disputing Errors and Inaccuracies

One of the vital steps for your credit score repair journey is to deal with errors and inaccuracies on your credit score score document. In this bankruptcy, we're capable of dive deep into the way of disputing the ones mistakes with the credit score score reporting organizations. Correcting the ones inaccuracies have to have a giant wonderful effect to your credit score score rating, so it's miles vital to recognize the nuances of the dispute system.

Section 5.1: The Importance of Disputing Errors

Credit report errors can upward thrust up for various motives, which include statistics access mistakes thru lenders or inaccuracies in reporting. These errors can drag down your credit score score score and limit your economic opportunities. That's why disputing them is a vital step on your credit restore plan.

Disputing mistakes serves numerous key abilities:

1. Improving Your Credit Score: Correcting inaccuracies can cause a enormous boom on your credit score score.

2. Accessing Better Financial Opportunities: Accurate credit rating rating evaluations are crucial for favorable mortgage phrases and reduce hobby expenses.

3. Protecting Your Identity: Resolving inaccuracies permits shield you in opposition to identity theft or fraud.

Section five.2: Gathering Documentation

Before starting a dispute, it is crucial to accumulate all of the important documentation to help your claims. This documentation can embody:

1. Credit Reports: Copies of your credit score rating reports from all three important credit score score rating reporting organizations.

2. Proof of Error: Any evidence that shows the inaccuracies to your credit record, which incorporates fee receipts or correspondence with lenders.

three. Dispute Letters: Well-crafted dispute letters outlining the specific mistakes you have identified.

Section 5.Three: Writing Effective Dispute Letters

Crafting nicely-based totally dispute letters is a critical part of the approach. These letters characteristic your formal conversation with the credit score reporting businesses, and they need to be clean, concise, and backed with the aid of proof. Here's a breakdown of what to encompass:

1. Your Personal Information: Start the letter along with your name, cope with, and Social Security quantity.

2. Identify the Errors: Clearly kingdom the inaccuracies you've got recognized for your credit score document.

Reference the specific devices you're disputing.

3. Provide Supporting Documentation: Attach copies of any proof that permits your dispute. Be sure to hold the precise documents for your information.

four. Request Correction: Clearly kingdom that you are soliciting for the elimination or correction of the inaccuracies.

5. Be Polite and Professional: Maintain a respectful and expert tone at a few diploma inside the letter.

6. Certified Mail: Send the dispute letter thru licensed mail with a move lower back receipt requested to hold a file of your communication.

Section five.Four: The Credit Reporting Agency's Investigation

After receiving your dispute letter, the credit score rating reporting enterprise organization (Equifax, Experian, or TransUnion) has 30 days to investigate your claims. During this era, they may touch the creditor or lender that said the statistics in question. If the creditor confirms that the statistics is correct, the item will stay for your report.

If the research effects in a change or removal of the disputed item, the credit score rating score reporting company will ship you an updated credit score score record reflecting the modifications.

Section five.Five: Follow-Up and Persistence

If the credit rating reporting agency does now not solve the dispute to your want, you have the right to request a reinvestigation or dispute the object yet again. Be persistent in your efforts to correct inaccuracies and maintain to offer evidence to guide your claims.

Disputing mistakes may be a time-consuming process, but it is a crucial step in your credit score restore adventure. By understanding the technique, providing proof, and being persistent, you can effectively task inaccuracies in your credit score score document and paintings inside the direction of a more accurate and favorable credit records. In the imminent chapters, we're capable of find out techniques for managing debt, constructing immoderate best credit score score, and maintaining healthful credit score score after repair.

Chapter 14: Paying Down Debt

Dealing with wonderful money owed is a critical aspect of your credit score repair adventure. High ranges of debt, particularly credit rating card debt, ought to have a massive terrible effect in your credit score rating score rating. In this monetary wreck, we are going to find out techniques for coping with and lowering your debt to beautify your credit score rating profile and common economic fitness.

Section 6.1: Assessing Your Current Debt Situation

Before you may create an effective debt reduction plan, you need a clean picture of your cutting-edge-day debt scenario. Here's what you must do:

1. Compile a List of Debts: Make a list of all of your outstanding debts, collectively with credit score rating score gambling playing cards, personal loans, pupil loans, medical payments, and every other monetary obligations.

2. Gather Account Information: Collect facts about every debt, in conjunction with the contemporary stability, hobby fee, minimum month-to-month fee, and the creditor's touch statistics.

three. Review Credit Card Balances: Pay close to interest to your credit score rating rating card balances and the percentage of available credit score score you've got used. High credit score score rating card usage can harm your credit score score rating.

Section 6.2: Creating a Budget and Financial Plan

Developing a finances is an vital step in handling and lowering your debt. Your fee range will assist you allocate charge range for debt repayment at the identical time as making sure you meet your extraordinary economic duties. Consider these budgeting steps:

1. List Your Income and Expenses: Document your month-to-month profits and all prices,

together with hire or loan, utilities, groceries, transportation, and enjoyment.

2. Identify Areas to Cut Costs: Analyze your spending to apprehend areas wherein you could cut returned and allocate extra fee variety toward debt reimbursement.

three. Prioritize Debt Payments: Determine how a whole lot you can manage to pay for to pay within the course of your debts every month, prioritizing excessive-hobby debts or those with the smallest balances for quicker payoff.

4. Emergency Fund: Allocate a part of your finances for an emergency fund to cowl sudden fees and prevent the want to rely upon credit rating score playing playing cards.

Section 6.Three: Reducing Debt Through Various Strategies

Once you've got got a budget in vicinity, you can rent severa techniques to lessen your debt efficiently:

1. Snowball Method: Focus on paying off the smallest debt first while making minimum bills on specific debts. As each debt is paid off, you roll its price into the subsequent smallest debt.

2. Avalanche Method: Prioritize paying off the debt with the very first-rate interest rate. This approach saves you coins in the end, as you pay less hobby.

three. Debt Consolidation: Consider consolidating a couple of money owed right into a single, lower-hobby loan or credit score score card to simplify your bills and decrease interest expenses.

four. Debt Negotiation: Negotiate with lenders or series agencies for decrease settlements or greater attainable compensation terms. Be positive to get any agreements in writing.

5. Balance Transfers: Transfer immoderate-hobby credit score card balances to playing playing playing cards with low or zero interest

promotional intervals to preserve on hobby prices.

Section 6.Four: Making Consistent On-Time Payments

Timely bills are crucial for enhancing your credit rating score. Be disciplined about making bills on time, as this detail appreciably affects your credit score rating.

1. Set up reminders or automatic bills to make certain you in no manner skip over a due date.

2. Consider growing an emergency fund to avoid relying on credit score score playing gambling playing cards for sudden expenses.

three. Contact your lenders in case you're experiencing financial problem to explore options for short remedy.

Section 6.5: Tracking and Celebrating Progress

Regularly display screen your debt bargain improvement and have fun milestones along the manner. This continues you stimulated and encourages you to paste for your plan.

1. Use a debt cut charge calculator or app to song your development.

2. Celebrate paying off individual debts thru acknowledging your achievements.

Reducing your debt is a massive step toward improving your credit score score and attaining financial balance. By assessing your contemporary-day debt state of affairs, growing a finances, and using effective debt reduction strategies, you can little by little art work inside the path of a debt-unfastened future. In the approaching chapters, we are going to discover techniques for constructing satisfactory credit score score, facts credit score repair criminal guidelines and rights, and maintaining a healthful credit score rating profile after your maintenance are whole.

Building Positive Credit

Repairing your credit rating rating is not just about addressing horrible gadgets to your credit score score document; it's also about building a brilliant credit score rating history that could help offset past troubles and enhance your normal creditworthiness. In this bankruptcy, we're going to discover strategies for putting in place and improving your nice credit score data.

www.ingramcontent.com/pod-product-compliance
Lightning Source LLC
Chambersburg PA
CBHW071218210326
41597CB00016B/1862